From *Wichita: The Magic City* by Craig Miner–

"Not only were the buildings going, but so were memories of the times when those structures were Wichita." In 1890, J.C. South of Wichita "…expressed the opinion that a local museum of some sort was needed. 'Who shall preserve these memories?.... The men who knew Jesse Chisholm, who listened with mingled emotions to the first church bell of the Arkansas valley, or who hunted buffalo from this starting point, are yearly growing fewer.' …Thirteen years later, Kos Harris, who had done more than his share in preserving local history, expressed a similar opinion. Harris suggested forming an historical society, even if the people in it had time and budget enough to do nothing more than bind old newspapers. For it was clear to Harris at least that Wichita was in 1903 fast becoming a wholly different place. It was already a major regional center and would become larger and more diverse in the future — more in need and less in command of the data of its own origin. 'Facts are fleeting,' Harris said, 'even among the denizens of a town … IN THE WHIRLIGIG OF TIME.'"

Wichita-Sedgwick County Historical Museum

Publication of

IN THE WHIRLIGIG OF TIME: PAGES FROM WICHITA HISTORY
has been made possible by a gift from the family of
Dr. Edward Nelson Tihen

The photographs and illustrations in this book include
images from the **Edward N. Tihen Collection** at
The Wichita-Sedgwick County Historical Museum

Library of Congress Catalog Card Number: 95-078685

ISBN 0-9621250-2-4

Copyright 1996 by
The Wichita-Sedgwick County Historical Museum, 204 S. Main, Wichita, Kansas 67202.
This publication may not be reproduced, stored in a retrieval system or transmitted in whole or in part,
in any form by any means, electronic, mechanical, photocopying, recording, or otherwise,
without prior permission of The Wichita-Sedgwick County Historical Museum.

Design and Composition by Sullivan LithoGraphics
115 South Handley, Wichita, Kansas 67213

Printed in the United States of America

DEDICATION

Wichita lost a prominent physician, an avid collector, and an authority on Wichita history and transportation with the death of Dr. Edward Nelson Tihen on April 24, 1991. It is with a deep feeling of respect and admiration that I pay tribute to this very special man.

Dr. Tihen was the sort of physician one would have loved to have had: kind and considerate. And, if a patient liked to talk about local history or transportation, that would have been part of the office call.

For Ed Tihen – a third-generation physician practicing in Sedgwick County – going into the medical field was a family tradition. His grandfather, Herman B. Tihen, practiced in Andale for 40 years. A great-uncle, Father J. Henry Tihen, was instrumental in the development of St. Francis Hospital, persuading the Sisters of the Sorrowful Mother to come from St. Louis in 1889 to make the hospital their mission. His father, Henry Nelson Tihen, practiced in Wichita for 51 years and was one of the founders of the Wichita Clinic, which opened January 2, 1948. In years following, other family members were Clinic physicians, including Ed's cousin, Philip W. Russell; his brother-in-law, Paul J. Uhlig; and Paul's son, Paul Nelson Uhlig.

Practicing medicine with his father was Ed Tihen's dream. After completing a fellowship in internal medicine at the Mayo Clinic, he turned down an invitation to remain on staff and joined his father in the department of internal medicine at the Wichita Clinic in 1956.

Dr. Tihen was an active member of the Medical Society of Sedgwick County and, in 1967, was appointed to a three-year term on the Public Relations and Public Policy Commission. He served as vice-president of the Society in 1969 and was appointed to a three-year term on the Medical Services Commission in 1970. He also served as president of the Wichita-Sedgwick County Heart Association in 1966.

Health problems forced Dr. Tihen to retire early in 1984, but his retirement was a fruitful and interesting time for him and for everyone who knew him. He possessed a wealth of knowledge and enjoyed sharing his "finds" with his many friends in groups ranging from the Rotary Club and the Medical Society of Sedgwick County to the Wichita Postcard Club and The Wichita Bibliophiles.

Dr. Edward Nelson Tihen–
Medicine was his Profession;
Transportation, his Passion

Although a physician by profession, Ed Tihen was obsessed by another love, and that was transportation. As a boy, he was fascinated by all of it: ships and planes, cars and trains. But, his specialty was the street railway system. This interest could have stemmed from the trips the family took to Europe when his father was studying medicine in Vienna.

According to family members, "Dr. Tihen was extremely well-read and well-traveled and amazed his friends and family with his phenomenal memory. He was knowledgeable about a wide range of subjects, including science, medicine, history, geography, world affairs, genealogy and all forms of transportation."

Dr. Ernest Crow, a retired internist and cardiologist, met Ed Tihen while both were attending the University of Kansas in the early 1940s. Crow was in medical school, and Ed Tihen was a college student living in the same fraternity house. "Even then," said Crow, "Ed Tihen was considered the authority on railroad time tables."

In 1982, Dr. Tihen was invited to join The Wichita Bibliophiles, a small group of collectors of old and rare books, which had formed around 1932-1933. The doctor was host for the first time in February 1983, and his program was entitled "Frank Braynard's Passion." All the members knew that when Ed Tihen hosted a program, transportation would be the subject. His other programs included "Street Cars Run by Lightning" and "Lighter-than-Air Craft."

He also became an avid member of Friends of the Trolley. This organization's interest was in restoring car #255, which had been a part of Wichita's Birney Street Railway system from 1919 to 1935. To every meeting, Dr. Tihen would bring a unique photograph or some "tidbits" of information about Wichita's street railway system. In the Postcard Club, he enjoyed sharing both his personal collection and his expert advice. I remember the program "Ocean Liners" that he presented to the club on July 2, 1985, following his trip to England on the *Queen Elizabeth II.*

As indicated, Ed Tihen was also an authority on Wichita history. He was the only person I know to have read completely all of the Wichita newspapers ever published, a feat he accomplished during his retirement years. When asked any question about our city's history, he usually knew the answer off the top of his head. If not, he could find the answer in his vast collection of notes — it was merely a matter of time.

It was the doctor's desire to write about Wichita history, particularly a book dealing with the city's street railway system. Although he never had time to write a book, he was a great help to those who did. For example, he corrected errors for the second printing of *Peerless Princess of the Plains: Postcard Views of Early Wichita,* by Hal Ottaway, Hal Ross, and Jack Stewart; he authenticated the transportation section of *Reflections of Kansas,* by Frank Wood and Scott Daymond; and he helped authenticate the minutiae in *Wichita: The Magic City,* by Craig Miner.

In short, Edward Tihen was a remarkable man. When declining health forced him to give up his practice, he did not retire from his other interests. He never complained about his illness, but maintained a positive attitude and made the best of his situation.

I considered it an honor to be associated with Dr. Tihen, and my life has been blessed by knowing him. He was a great encouragement to me in all of my Wichita history projects, and it is a privilege to dedicate this book, a collection of writings on some of my favorite topics, to his memory.

– Beverly Henline

Articles

1. "Buffalo Bill" Mathewson Was the Marrying Kind 7
2. Builder S. G. Gribi: Wichita's Forgotten Pioneer 9
3. City's First "Fourth" Featured Parade, Speeches, Buffalo Feed 11
4. "With Women, Wonderful Wichita Wins" 13
5. Boomtime Banker L. D. Skinner Left Wichita a Better Place 15
6. Murdock's "Christmas Reverie" a Holiday Gem 17
7. This River City Had a "Music Man," Too 19
8. Grand Railroad Excursion Included Steamboat Jaunt 21
9. In 1885, Citizens Urged to Be Thankful for Wichita 23
10. Master Architect U. G. Charles Set His Sights on Wichita 25
11. Horses Were "One of the Family" a Hundred Years Ago 27
12. In Spite of Recent Bust, Christmas Spirit Boomed in 1896 29
13. First *Messiah* Production a Crowning Achievement 31
14. 1899 Street Fair and Carnival Set a Tradition in Motion 33
15. The Millers: Educator and Entertainer Extraordinaire 35
16. More Glimpses of People from Wichita's Past 37
17. In 1903, Mayor Proclaimed Observance of Memorial Day 39
18. 1904 Flood Left Devastation in Its Wake 41
19. Movie Actor Got His Start on Wichita Stage 43
20. "Mermaid" Made Waves in Riverside Park 45
21. Christmas of 1908 a Wichita Merchant's Dream 47
22. Lincoln's 100th Birthday an Occasion to Reminisce 49
23. "Kirby Castle" the Setting for Classic June Wedding 51
24. 1911 Jubilee Included Dramatic River Show 53
25. "Kansas Post Card Day" a Successful Campaign in 1912 55
26. Riverside's Park Villa: a Labor of Love 57
27. Halloween of Yesteryear Was Fun for All Ages 59
28. Balloon Race Thrust Wichita into National Spotlight 61
29. Drive to Motorize Fire Department Signaled End of Era 63
30. Helen Keller Made Lasting Impression on Wichita Audience 65
31. Henry Lassen Hailed as a "Public Utility" 67
32. Fountain Recalls Founding of the Wichita *Eagle* 69
33. Silent Screen Actress Dreamed of Wichita Movie Studio 71
34. A. A. Hyde Honored for Global Generosity 73
35. Christmas 1925 Ushered in "Buy Now, Pay Later" Scheme 75
36. Glorious Victory Arch Honored World War I Troops 77
37. In 1934, Many "Danced Off" Their Thanksgiving Dinner 79
38. William Boulton: No Ordinary Pony Express Rider 81
39. Charles Boulton Shared "Close Shave" with Radio Audience 83
40. Wichita's City Flag Displays Indian Symbols, National Colors 85
41. Wichita Boathouse Makes a Spectacular Comeback 87

PUBLISHER'S NOTE

Between 1990 and 1995, Wichita researcher and popular historian Beverly Henline was a regular contributor to *Active Aging*, a newsletter for senior citizens. Her colorful articles on people, places, customs, and events brought history to life for *Active Aging* readers, who looked forward each month to another absorbing episode. This book is a collection of 41 of those articles, which have been edited for publication, but for the most part are presented here in Beverly's own, informal style.

Except in those few instances where a fascinating story source fell into her hands, Beverly developed her topics by gleaning old issues of the local newspapers. The bulk of her material was found in editions of the Wichita *Eagle* and the Wichita *Beacon*, and any unattributed quotations contained in her writings were drawn from those sources. Until the time of his death, Beverly also consulted fellow researcher and Wichita history expert Dr. Edward N. Tihen when she needed more details or clarification of some point.

We were guided in our decision to publish these articles by our memory of Ed Tihen, his enthusiastic support for the preservation of Wichita's heritage, and his support of Beverly's endeavors. It was always a pleasure to work with Ed, and I know he would appreciate how grateful we are to Beverly for her tireless efforts to research the city's history and share her knowledge with the community. Of course, this book would not have been possible without the patience and generosity of Ed's family, whose backing has made it a project worthy of his memory.

Robert A. Puckett, Director
The Wichita-Sedgwick County Historical Museum

"Buffalo Bill" Mathewson Was the Marrying Kind

Much has been written about the career of William Mathewson, the original "Buffalo Bill." Many newspaper articles have dwelt on the subject of who received that title first, William Mathewson or William Cody. Very little has been written about his domestic life, however, in spite of the fact that he was a husband for 50 years and had three different wives.

A hunter and trader on the Kansas frontier, William Mathewson served as a scout for the United States Government and supplied buffalo meat for settlers. He owned trading posts on Cow Creek and Walnut Creek along the Santa Fe Trail.

On August 28, 1864, he married Elizabeth Inman, who the local history books say was the best representative of the pioneer women of Kansas. With Mathewson, Lizzie (as she was called by her family and friends) shared the dangers of the plains. She became an expert in the use of the knife and revolver, and many times stood by her husband's side fighting off Indian attacks on their home or camp.

The Mathewsons traded supplies to the Indians in return for furs and hides. Lizzie became quite successful as a trader and was known by the Indians as Marr Wissi ("Golden Hair"). Their name for William, whom they admired but dreaded, was Sinpah Zilbah ("Long-Bearded, Dangerous White Man").

While the couple lived on Walnut Creek, many army officers frequented their home. Guests included Generals Sherman, Canby, and Hancock, and Col. J. H. Leavenworth, the noted Indian agent. Henry M. Stanley, the Eastern journalist who later became a famous explorer in Africa, was also a guest. According to J. R. Mead's book *Hunting and Trading on the Great Plains, 1859-1875,* Stanley "spent a month or two at Mathewson's ranch, and the interesting letters which he wrote back were largely based on information given him by Mrs. Mathewson, a most notable and energetic lady, who was as well versed in the affairs of the plains as was her distinguished husband."

In addition to numerous wagons of government supplies, Mathewson rescued over 200 men, women, and children from death or capture, and his wife clothed and cared for them. Lizzie became a mother to the orphaned and friendless and showed kindness and generosity to those in need or distress.

William Mathewson was instrumental in the signing of several treaties with the Plains tribes, including the *Little Arkansas Peace Treaty* at 61st Street and North Seneca and the famous *Medicine Lodge Treaty*. The *Little Arkansas Peace Treaty* opened up this land for settlement.

Around 1868, the Mathewsons acquired 160 acres east of town[1] and built a log cabin. The cabin remained standing for many years after they built their two-story house.

Mathewson's close friend James R. Mead was also a hunter and trader on the frontier. When Mead's wife died in 1869, Lizzie Mathewson took over the care of his three small children (the fourth one had died shortly after Mrs. Mead). In 1873, Mead married Lizzie's sister, Lucy Inman, who had been his housekeeper. Thus, Mead and Mathewson became brothers-in-law.

Elizabeth Mathewson died October 1, 1885, at the age of 43. Ironically, she died at the Mead home, where Lucy was taking care of her. She left behind two children, Lucy, age 4, and William, age 2.

Lucy Mead cared for her sister's children until Mathewson remarried on May 11, 1886. His second wife was Caroline M. (Henshaw) Tarlton, a widow. The marriage lasted 23 years, until Caroline died in 1909.

In 1911, Mathewson purchased the Dr. Minick home[2] at 1047 North Market for his new bride, Olive Johnson. Olive, a close friend of Mathewson's, had been living with the Mead

Drawing of "Buffalo Bill" Mathewson's first wife, Elizabeth Inman, c. 1880.

Drawing of William "Buffalo Bill" Mathewson, c. 1880.

family. She was a stenographer in bankruptcy court for Judge Ferguson and was highly respected in the community. Olive died January 29, 1916, at age 38.

Six weeks later, on March 21, 1916, William Mathewson died. He was 86. It is interesting to note that he outlived all three of his wives, who are buried next to him at Highland Cemetery[3].

---
[1] the site many people will remember as "Mathewson's pasture"
[2] which still stands
[3] northwest corner of Ninth and Hillside

Builder S. G. Gribi: Wichita's Forgotten Pioneer

When thinking of the early settlers who shaped Wichita, names like Henry Schweiter, Darius Sales Munger, Marshall M. Murdock, and James R. Mead immediately spring to mind. Wichitans are reminded of their contributions almost daily by the buildings, streets, and parks that bear their names; and, their achievements are duly noted in the local history books. An exception is Samuel Gottlieb Gribi. For a reason unknown, this pioneer carpenter and builder is little remembered today, although he lived in Wichita and contributed to its growth for 56 years.

Samuel Gottlieb Gribi, better known as S. G. Gribi, was born March 27, 1844, in Buren, Switzerland. He learned the carpentry trade from the same foreman who trained his fellow countryman Henry Schweiter.

In 1868, at the age of 24, Gribi and his wife, Anna, emigrated to America and settled in Topeka, where he took a job working on the new Kansas statehouse. There, he met up with his old friend from home, Henry Schweiter, who was working on the same building. While constructing the statehouse, Gribi and Schweiter became close friends with John Davidson, Sr. (who would become another well-known Wichitan).

In the winter of 1869, Gribi, Schweiter, and a stone mason named Chris Kimmerle (who also came to Wichita) were hired to build a house near Topeka for Abram Burnett, Chief of the Pottawatomie Indians. During this time, William Greiffenstein (the "Father of Wichita") was "sparking the Chief's daughter," Catherine, and so visited Topeka often. While in town, Greiffenstein promoted Wichita and all its possibilities. As a result of his continual boasting, many people followed him here, including Catherine, who came as his bride.

In a developing town like Wichita, it was not hard for a builder to find a job. Like Schweiter, Davidson, and Kimmerle, Gribi was persuaded to put down roots in Wichita. Leaving his wife in Topeka, Gribi moved to Wichita in May of 1870. According to his recollections, when he arrived in town: "There were no streets. The town site was grown up in very tall grass. The cattle had cut trails through the grass and these were used by the children going to and from town. The grass was higher than the heads of the little girls who followed the paths to market. There were no meat markets in Wichita then. We ate buffalo meat and fish. We had a glorious time in those early days. Very few of us had very much capital, but we had plenty of good muscle and determination."

Because Greiffenstein was promoting his area, he gave Gribi a lot in the 300 block of North Market Street. After building a house – a simple one-room structure made from cottonwood lumber – Gribi sent for his wife and child. According to her obituary, "Mrs. Gribi, with a baby in her arms, drove a wagon from Topeka to Wichita…, She made the trip alone with the exception of her baby and often spoke in later years of the long journey."

In February of 1871, Gribi was outside planting sycamore trees in his yard when he had to stop because bullets were flying thick and fast in the vicinity. United States Government troops were in Wichita to capture Jack Ledford, a man wanted for robbery and murder involving a government pack train. Ledford, at the time, was proprietor of the Harris House, a new hotel that William Greiffenstein had built. Ledford died in the hail of bullets, and Gribi never finished planting the last of his trees.

"He was pre-eminently a builder." Gribi took pride in what he did, and everything that he constructed was made with great skill and workmanship. Not only did Gribi contract for residences, but he also built schoolhouses and business buildings, including the first Bitting Building. During his early days in Wichita, he also contracted for buildings in Newton, Kansas, riding home each Saturday night on an Indian pony.

In the 1877 map of Wichita, Gribi advertised as a contractor and builder, located on the corner of First and Water Streets. During the height of the boom in 1887, Gribi built a new office building at that location[1].

One of the last projects Gribi undertook during his active years in the construction business was the Missouri Pacific depot on Douglas Avenue between Wichita and Water Streets. It was formally opened on January 1, 1901.

Portrait of Samuel Gottlieb Gribi, c. 1888.

In addition to building, Gribi was known for his civic involvement. He was a member of the City Council in 1897 and 1898, representing the first ward. He was also a member of the German Lutheran Church, the Elks Lodge, and the Sedgwick County Pioneer Society. At the time of his death in 1926, at age 82, he was still active in business, a vice-president of the American Building and Loan Company, and an insurance adjustor.

Everyone who knew Gribi "esteemed him and was honored in calling him a friend." His obituary in the Wichita *Eagle* said: "His loss is a great one to this community. He helped to build it, and into its life he cast more than an ordinary contribution, a contribution of kindliness that was outstanding and the influence of which will be carried down through the years by all who had the good fortune to know him."

Samuel Gottlieb Gribi and his wife, Anna, are buried at Wichita's historic Maple Grove Cemetery[2]. A grandson and namesake, Samuel G. Gribi, was interviewed by the *Eagle* in 1933, when he was in town for his grandmother's funeral. The paper reported that the aviator from Chickasha, Oklahoma, Samuel G. Gribi, "probably was the last American acquaintance who saw Jimmy Mattern, 'round-the-world flier,' who has been missing since he took off from Siberia for Alaska. It was at Omsk, Russia, that Gribi last saw Mattern, when his plane landed and taxied up to within hailing distance of a plane the former had rented."

---

[1] later the site of the Colorado Derby Building
[2] northeast corner of Ninth and Hillside

Note: Unattributed quotations in this article appeared in the Wichita *Eagle* in 1912 and the Wichita *Eagle* and Wichita *Beacon* in 1926.

City's First "Fourth" Featured Parade, Speeches, Buffalo Feed

"Before Wichita had a newspaper, and when the town was made up of a dozen dirt-roof shacks, they had a Fourth of July celebration," reported the El Dorado *Republican*. Sedgwick County had only been organized for four months, and it was just 17 days before the 124 property owners would sign the incorporation papers to make Wichita a town in 1870, that the community celebrated Independence Day.

At the time, the *Walnut Valley Times* of El Dorado, in Butler County, was the only general newspaper serving the area. On June 10, it reported that Wichita was situated at the junction of the Little and Big Arkansas Rivers; there was lots of fertile soil, and "they were looking for two or three railroads to build a large city."

There were then 30 houses, four dry goods and grocery stores, a bakery, a drug store, a saloon, two physicians, a harness and bootmaker, a blacksmith, and two sawmills. In addition, said promoters, "We also have a good meat market, and abundance of the finest fish are brought to town daily for sale, caught out of the Arkansas river."

The Presbyterians and Episcopals had already organized, and the Methodists were to organize soon. Some buildings were made from sod, some were picket covered with earth, and a few were made from lumber, which was scarce at that time.

At least two women ran their own businesses: Mrs. Matilda Drew's millinery shop carried a large supply of ladies' fancy dress goods, and Mrs. Catherine McCarty (mother of "Billy the Kid") owned the City Laundry on North Main Street, where folks could have their linen made clean. Mrs. McCarty was the only female to sign the incorporation papers for Wichita, because only she owned her property.

For those traveling to Wichita for the Fourth of July celebration, there were plenty of good accommodations for both ladies and gents. Henry Vigus, the harness maker, "with his estimable lady, keep hotel, and supply the wants of the hungry or weary traveler." Darius Sales Munger and wife, Julia, kept the Munger House, which was known as "the traveler's home." Munger also had maps and charts showing the location of most of the land in the settled portions of the county.

One of the earliest known photos of Wichita, dated June 1870.

"Any one can receive the best accommodations at J. W. Vandervoorts on Main Street," it was said. And, the new Wichita House, a two-story frame hotel and the largest in town, had just been completed by William Greiffenstein. At the time, Greiffenstein was buying lots on Douglas Avenue and giving them away to those desiring to build there.

July 4, 1870, began with the firing of 37[1] guns at sunrise. At 10:00 a.m., a procession formed in front of the Wichita House (northwest corner of Third and Main). It was headed up by a string band and followed by 37 young ladies riding bronco, the Good Templar Order (Lodge), the Park City delegation, the Wichita delegation, the Cow Skin delegation, and the Spring Creek delegation.

David L. Payne was grand marshal. The committee for the celebration included Henry VanTrees, Girard H. Smith, John Meagher, John Hunter, and Phares C. Hubbard. Officers for the day were Judge Reuben Riggs, president; T. S. Floyd, 1st assistant marshal; William Yanks, 2nd assistant marshal; and T. W. Ransom, 3rd assistant marshal.

The parade marched down Main Street to Eli P. Waterman's grove[2], where music, speeches, and food awaited.

Leading the crowd in prayer was the Reverend Dr. Boggs of the First Presbyterian Church. The string band entertained with music, and *The Declaration of Independence* was read by Milton Stewart. Orations by Dr. Deering and James R. Mead and a speech by William Jay, Esq., of Emporia, were heard.

Dinner, which was free to all, had as its main course barbecued buffalo — the product of a two-day guided buffalo hunt just prior to the celebration. Plenty of rain had created a bountiful harvest of fresh fruits and vegetables, providing guests with "the best luxuries that the country can produce."

In the evening, a grand ball was held at the Wichita House, which concluded the day's activities.

Fourth of July celebrations in Wichita have come a long way since 1870, but as the *Walnut Valley Times* reported on the first such occasion: "We could not ask for a more pleasant gathering; if this be Kansas, we are content to trust her future with the people."

---

[1] to signify the number of states in the Union
[2] the area south and west of Central and Waco to the river

Note: Unattributed quotations in this article were taken from write-ups published in the *Walnut Valley Times* of El Dorado in 1870.

Although women played an important role in Wichita's early development, they are more difficult to research than men, and most of them are not written up in local history books. While there isn't enough information available to produce a story on each one, it is fitting that some of their individual achievements be acknowledged.

Even when Wichita was in its infancy, it was not uncommon for a woman to own her own business. Both Mrs. M. M. Drew and Mrs. E. R. Newcomb advertised in Wichita's first paper, the Wichita *Vidette*, in 1870 – Mrs. Drew as a dealer in staple and fancy dry goods and notions, and Mrs. Newcomb as a fashionable dressmaker, with particular attention given to dressmaking, shirtmaking, coats, pants, and vests made to order. And, in 1875, Mrs. Emily Buser operated an embroidery school, where ladies and girls were taught all kinds of fancy work, including silk embroidery, canvas embroidery, crochet, knitting, tatting, and netting. She also dressed hair.

"With Women, Wonderful Wichita Wins"

During the boom period of the 1880s, Harriet Pearl Skinner, a sister of the prominent banker L. D. Skinner, was involved in Wichita's social circles and appeared in many local theatrical productions. Her family left Wichita during the financial bust of the 1890s, and she later moved to New York with her banker husband, Samuel McRoberts. Pearl, as she was known in Wichita, wrote children's stories and magazine reviews. Her books included *Boys Who Became Famous Men: Stories of the Childhood of Poets, Artists, and Musicians; A Christian Crieth unto Israel: Twelve Songs;* and *Every Christian: Poems.* She was also director of the American Bible Society and a member of the National Bible Institute.

In February of 1887, a group of Wichita women filed a charter for a corporation with a capital stock of $100,000 under the name of The Wichita Syndicate. The directors – all property owners interested in Wichita's growth – included Ella Davis Hull, Sallie Toler, Martha S. Collings, Ella Glenn Sheilds, and Elizabeth M. Packer. The purpose of the corporation was to buy and sell real estate, erect buildings, and loan money. Its slogan was "With Women, Wonderful Wichita Wins."

About the same time, Mrs. L. T. Ewen of Wichita composed a beautiful piece of music entitled *The Wichita Waltzes*, which was arranged for full orchestra and dedicated to the Eagle Rifles Association[1]. The number was first performed in 1888 at a local military kirmesse[2] by the orchestra under the leadership of Professor George F. Berkimer at the Crawford Opera House[3]. The festival was produced under the auspices of the ladies' guild as a benefit for St. John's Episcopal Church, 402 N. Topeka.

In 1895, a roving, petticoated evangelist, the Reverend Ella F. Tharp, came to Wichita to hold a service. During her stay in the city, she performed a wedding for a young couple from Bentley, Kansas, in the parlor of the Keystone Hotel, 228-1/2 North Main. According to a Wichita *Eagle* report, "she did the job as gracefully and easily as any man."

After her graduation from Fairmount College[4] in 1901, Wichitan Molly Warren Wilcox went on to the University of Chicago and Harvard University before returning to teach English at Wichita High School. She became one of the first women editors in Kansas, working as an editorial writer for the Wichita *Beacon* and the Wichita *Eagle*. She also owned *The Democrat* for several years. Molly's enthusiasm for journalism probably stemmed from her father, Major Park S. Warren, a pioneer Kansas newspaperman.

Night view of lighted promotional sign over Douglas at St. Francis, c. 1910.

In the early 1900s, The Keister Ladies' Tailoring College and School of Dressmaking was quite popular. "The Keister System is by far the best of the many and varied systems of dress cutting" reported the Wichita *Eagle* in 1908. An advertisement in the same paper read: "We teach all branches of cutting, fitting and sewing. Graduates assisted to positions." Mrs. Emma A. Marchino, Mrs. Florence Lutz, and Mrs. Priscilla Mantz were all managers of the school, which opened at 207 East First and later moved into the Butts Building[5]. In an article on the art of dressmaking which appeared in the

Eagle in 1920, Mrs. Mantz explained that many people were learning dressmaking "in all its branches and the making of wool suits is no longer a lost art to the average woman with time to spare for the building of the garment."

About the same time, Mrs. Monnie Moore Latham, a Wichita journalist, wrote a song entitled *Where My Picture Hangs Upon the Parlor Wall*, which was published in 1910 by the Haviland Publishing Company of New York. To "illustrate" the song, slides of Wichita, produced from photographs by Homer T. Harden, were projected on a screen during performance of the number. The production was first booked in Wichita and then throughout Kansas and Missouri. Within a few months, Mrs. Latham's song, accompanied by picturesque slide views of Wichita, was being sung by "high class" artists on the stages of New York music halls. She had a local publishing company, under the direction of Webb Long, produce an orchestration for her song, and the number was first played by Mrs. Bamberger's Orchestra for the traveling men's banquet held at the Hamilton Hotel[6].

In 1922, the Wichita *Eagle* interviewed Le Fern Niles and Mrs. Kate Gray regarding the wardrobe that Mrs. Gray, a local dressmaker, was currently working on for Miss Niles, a film actress from the West Coast. Miss Niles had spent most of her early life in Wichita and knew the talented Mrs. Gray, who made many of the clothes that she wore in her films. In talking to reporters, the seamstress said she had "in the making five gowns, most of them evening designs, for the western visitor. All of them will be used in pictures that will be filmed by the Lasky Corporation[7], of which Miss Niles is a member." During the interview, Miss Niles explained why a California-based actress employed a dressmaker from Wichita: "I have had many gowns designed, but no one in California can come up to Mrs. Gray."

---

[1] a military organization
[2] or kirmess, variation of kermis: a church festival; a fair held usually for charitable purposes
[3] built in 1887 on the southwest corner of Topeka and William
[4] predecessor to Wichita State University
[5] located at 145-149 North Lawrence (now Broadway)
[6] located at 238-244 South Main
[7] The Lasky Corporation later became Paramount Pictures.

Wichita's Skinner/Lee House Museum, which once welcomed the public at 637 North Topeka, is now only a memory – at least at that location. Today, the house sits at 1344 North Topeka and is privately owned by a family committed to preserving its character.

The house was built by Lysander DeWitt Skinner, a man whose name deserves credit in Wichita's history along with pioneers like J. R. Mead, William Greiffenstein, and Marsh Murdock. L. D. Skinner played a tremendous role in the development of Wichita from the time he came here in 1880 until his bank closed in 1894.

In 1880, Skinner was working for a bank in Creston, Iowa. He was sent "to Kansas with instructions to select a location for a new bank; and, of course, when he looked over the field, the young financier selected Wichita." Here, he established the Kansas State Bank, which grew under his leadership as cashier to become one of the city's leading banking institutions. It was located on the southwest corner of Main and Douglas – an intersection that became the most prestigious in terms of activity of any west of Chicago during the boom period of the 1880s.

Boomtime Banker L. D. Skinner Left Wichita a Better Place

In 1886, the Kansas State Bank became the State National Bank. Many prominent and substantial businessmen and capitalists were connected with the bank, including John B. Carey, J. P. Allen, Dr. Andrew Fabrique, P. V. Healy, Kos Harris, and Peter Getto. The local newspapers sang Skinner's praises: "Mr. Skinner is a young man in years, but there are few who are more capable of grasping the financial questions of the day. The State Bank has grown up under his management to be one of the best banks in the west, and the returns to the stockholders have been satisfactory. Mr. Skinner indulges in no speculations, but attends strictly to his banking business."

Probably one of the highest honors paid Skinner was to be chosen the banker to represent this area at the World's Congress of Bankers and Financiers at the Chicago World's Fair in 1893. The Wichita *Daily Eagle's* appraisal said: "The selection was a good one, as Mr. Skinner is not only well equipped from every standpoint to participate in the deliberations of such an important assembly, but he is a young man compared with the majority of those who will be present, thus typifying the youth and activity of the financial and business interests of the Arkansas valley."

L. D. Skinner was not only a banker, but also a community leader who contributed to many areas of Wichita's growth. He was a member of the Board of Trade, the Boat Club, and the Eagle Rifles[1]. He served as treasurer for the Wichita Creamery and as a trustee for Wichita University (an early school on College Hill that was a victim of the real estate bust of the early 1890s)[2]. And, he promoted a number of city improvements, including the street railway system.

A 1980 rendering of the Skinner/Lee house by Lloyd Foltz, commissioned by the Wichita Victorian Society.

Soon after Skinner moved to Wichita, he sent for his new bride, Margaret Butler. Because they were a close-knit family, L. D.'s parents, Lydia and Anson; his brother, Sherman; and his four sisters, Ida, May, Minnie, and Pearl, soon followed him to Wichita. The entire family became active in the community. They all took part in social gatherings and, each in his or her own way, made an impact on Wichita.

When Skinner's father passed away, L. D., being the oldest, kept the family together. In 1886, he purchased two lots on North Topeka on which to build houses – one for his mother, brother, and sisters, and the other for himself, his wife, and their two children, Lucille and Paul. The family home was at 635 North Topeka and Skinner's home was at 637 North Topeka.

Together, the two homes were a hub of activity, and the society pages were filled with articles about the Skinners' gracious hospitality. At Christmastime in 1887, Mrs. L. D. Skinner entertained with a luncheon for 51 ladies, including Mrs. M. W. Levy, Mrs. J. O. Davidson, Mrs. R. P. Murdock, and Mrs. N. F. Neiderlander. "The residence on North Topeka

Avenue was the rendezvous of the elite of society throughout the afternoon," reported the papers. And, in 1891, at the house next door, Mr. Skinner's mother entertained ladies at a four o'clock tea. Included among her guests were Mrs. M. M. Murdock, Mrs. David Winters, Mrs. J. P. Allen, and Mrs. F. G. Smythe. That same year, Skinner's sister Pearl hosted a party out-of-doors on the two adjoining lawns. According to a report in the Wichita *Mirror*, guests enjoyed tennis, croquet, and other outdoor games and feasted on a bounteous lunch. "The merry makers spent the evening hours with music, fun and flash light photography."

Unfortunately, the boom could not last, and the market collapsed. Although it was one of the last in Wichita to fold as a result of the bust, Skinner's bank closed in 1894, and he and his family moved to Chicago.

In 1900, Mrs. Carlton O. Lee, a widow, and her daughter, Myrta, purchased the L. D. Skinner house. Mrs. Lee passed away in 1916, but Myrta continued to live in the house until a few years before she died in 1978, just shy of 103 years of age.

During their 78 years of ownership, the Lees attempted no major improvements, but left the house virtually intact. Although a great many repairs were needed, the house was ideal for historical purposes because it had never been altered. It was purchased by the Wichita Victorian Society and served as a museum during the 1980s. But, because of rising maintenance costs and falling membership, the house soon became a liability, and the Society could no longer manage it. In 1991, it was sold to Don and Marlene Chew, a caring Wichita couple. With the help of Mennonite Housing and the Midtown Citizens Association, the house was moved to an historic district just a few blocks north of its original site, and the Chews have since restored it.

L. D. Skinner lives on not only through the house, but also through a street named after him. It is fitting that Skinner Street is near the "banking" streets in Wichita: Gold, Silver, Exchange Place, and Mt. Vernon[3].

_____

[1] a military organization
[2] not to be confused with Fairmount College, which later became Wichita University, then Wichita State University
[3] Mt. Vernon was originally named Levy Street after M. W. Levy, a banker and close friend of Skinner's.

Note: Unattributed quotations in this article were taken from issues of the Wichita *Eagle* and the Wichita *Beacon* during the 1880s and 1890s.

Perhaps the most influential man in Wichita's early development was Col. Marshall M. Murdock, founder and editor of the Wichita *Eagle*. He is still remembered today through his home (a part of Old Cowtown Museum), the Murdock memorial drinking fountain (northeast corner of Third and Main), and Murdock Street.

In 1884, the newspaperman took time to reflect on his family's Christmas Day. He and his wife, Victoria, had spent the day with friends, while daughters Kate and Pearl and son Victor had plans of their own. His young son Marcellus was left at home with the family servant. About mealtime, Murdock's father, Thomas, paid a surprise visit and spent the day with grandson Marcellus.

Colonel Murdock wrote about this event in his paper, and the article was reprinted in later years. It "breathes the spirit of the day," and is worth repeating here.

Murdock's "Christmas Reverie" a Holiday Gem

Christmas Reverie

There were many fine spreads, many rich repasts discussed Christmas day in the homes of Wichita, but we know of one at which were present only a baby boy and an old man. The handsome, bright little mistress of the kitchen who hails from the land of Hamlet, that land so prolific of olden-time noble feasts, had dressed and trussed a royal specimen of the real emblematic bird of America. The two sisters of the household had gone to spend the day with friends in another city, the oldest son had boyish engagements of his own to meet, and the father and mother were enjoying the hospitalities of friends down on south Main street, and the pretty cook and baby boy were thus left the sole occupants of that home – the one to serve and the other the sole monarch of the feast which had been prepared with such care.

It so happened that the aged grandfather, who had arrived on the train during the night before, made his appearance just before the turkey was taken from the oven and these lone two sat down to the feast together, the one with his white bib beneath his dimpled chin, and the other with his white beard upon his breast, grand sire and grand son; the one with the frosts of seventy-two winters resting upon his head, the other with the bright suns of but two summers upon him; one with his life all before him, the other with that conflict all behind him; one in his beauty fresh from the hands of the infinite, the other in patience waiting to be received back to that same loving hand; the bud and the full ripened fruit.

Upon the return of the inmates of that home, as were falling the shades of evening, the soft light of the fire revealed these two heads close, lovingly together over a holiday number of the "Babe and the Manger." That these dear heads formed a touching picture for at least one may be readily believed, and that one the writer of these lines, who is the son of the one and the father of the other.

Marshall Murdock may not have written about another Christmas quite like the one of 1884, but the local newspapers often reported his Christmas entertainments. As recorded by the Wichita *Sunday Growler*, Christmas at the Eagle Roost[1] in 1887 included a dinner party given by the Murdocks for Col. and Mrs. Milton Stewart, who had just returned from an extended European tour. The large drawing room was decorated with old English holly, and a Christmas tree was illuminated with candles. In the center of the folding doors was a large Star of Bethlehem.

Photo of Col. Marshall M. Murdock, founder and editor of the Wichita Eagle, c. 1895.

Mrs. Murdock was "a hostess of rare ability, and the dinner, served in courses, was the perfection of the art of dining." According to the paper, her Egyptian-themed menu included:

Rameses Soup
"Nile of America" Ale
Oysters on the Half Shell
Salt Fish   Fresh Fish   Celery
Meleagris (fowl)   Claret   Pontet Canet
Cranberry Sauce
Escalloped Oysters   Potatoes a la Irish   French Peas
Virginia Partridge   Champagne
Current Jelly
Salad, Mayonnaise Dressing
Cheese and Crackers
Pyramid Pudding   Brandy Sauce
Cherps Ice
Cakes   Fruits
Coffee
Sphinx Cheroet

A year later, Colonel Stewart returned from Europe with a gift for Murdock: a pearl paper knife fashioned by a descendant of Abraham in Bethlehem. It was this gift that inspired Marsh Murdock to write another famous Christmas editorial, "The Light of That Night," which appeared in the *Eagle* on Christmas Day in 1888 and has been reprinted almost every Christmas since then.

---

[1] the Murdock home, northwest corner of Murdock and St. Francis

This River City Had a "Music Man," Too

Music has always played an important role in Wichita's development. When one thinks of the city's early music houses, orchestras, and opera houses, the name Thomas Shaw comes to mind.

Shaw was born near Morris, Illinois, and eventually went into the music business there. On July 4, 1884, he arrived in Wichita on the Santa Fe. When asked years later why he came to Wichita, Shaw replied, "As every business man knows, a lack of competition drives away all incentive for progress.... Morris was about as big as it would ever be, so that there was no chance for growth."

Initially, Shaw bought out the music stock of Hiram W. Kendle at 113 East Douglas. Later, he bought out Ion Arnold's stock and moved to 129 North Main. In 1902, he relocated his store to 132 North Main.

The Thomas Shaw Music Store carried sheet music, sewing machines, bicycles, talking machines, and all kinds of musical instruments. In the sewing machine department, customers were assisted by knowledgeable employees who showed them the best makes and latest improvements. The bicycle department offered models by Columbia, Victor, Hartford, and 210, as well as many less expensive brands. Piano buyers could choose from Emerson, Mason and Hamlin, Dobson, and Decker Brothers pianos. Customer services included expert piano tuning for $2.50 and repairs on the instruments.

Shaw's motto was "small profits and big volume." Customers in Kansas, Colorado, and Oklahoma were assured by Shaw that "we never allow anybody at any time or place to undersell us," and that "terms to suit" were readily available. Additional emphasis was on the special attention given to mail orders.

From the start, Shaw advertised heavily in the local newspapers. The heart of his message was: "Thomas Shaw can give you a better piano or organ for the money than any man that travels. Don't buy till you see him....We import our Band Instruments direct from Europe and can furnish you anything in this line as cheap as any house in America, and less than any Western houses."

On February 1, 1887, the Wichita *Daily Eagle*, reported: "Thos. Shaw is still rolling out the pianos. He has just sold County Attorney Jones a celebrated Decker Bros.; Dr. A. H. Wendall a Decker Bros.; and J. R. Gandolfo another fine Upright for his hotel; Nicholas Dodge a fine Decker Bros.; Gants & Mahan an Emerson; R. C. Deam a Mason & Hamlin; Prof. E. H. Fitch a Dobson; C. Schober a Decker Bros.; Thomas Jewell a Decker Bros."

At Christmastime in 1895, Shaw's advertisements listed the following as gift suggestions: "Pianos: new, $200 and up; second-hand, $25 to $100. Music boxes: first-class, less than cost to manufacture; small ones, for the children, 35 cents and up. Jew's Harp: 5 cents. Zithers: $6.00 and up."

An 1896 store brochure advertised a number of musical instruments: mouth harp, violin, mandolin, square piano, upright piano, cottage organ, guitar, accordion, and even a child's tin horn. But, it was the Everett piano, claimed the brochure, that "was the symbol of the discerning 'musical' elect."

Besides being a music dealer, Shaw managed an orchestra and earned the title "The Music Man." "Shaw's orchestra is prepared to furnish music for parties, weddings, etc.," ran the ads. For nearly three decades, the Thomas Shaw Orchestra played engagements in opera houses, private homes, parks, and at the store.

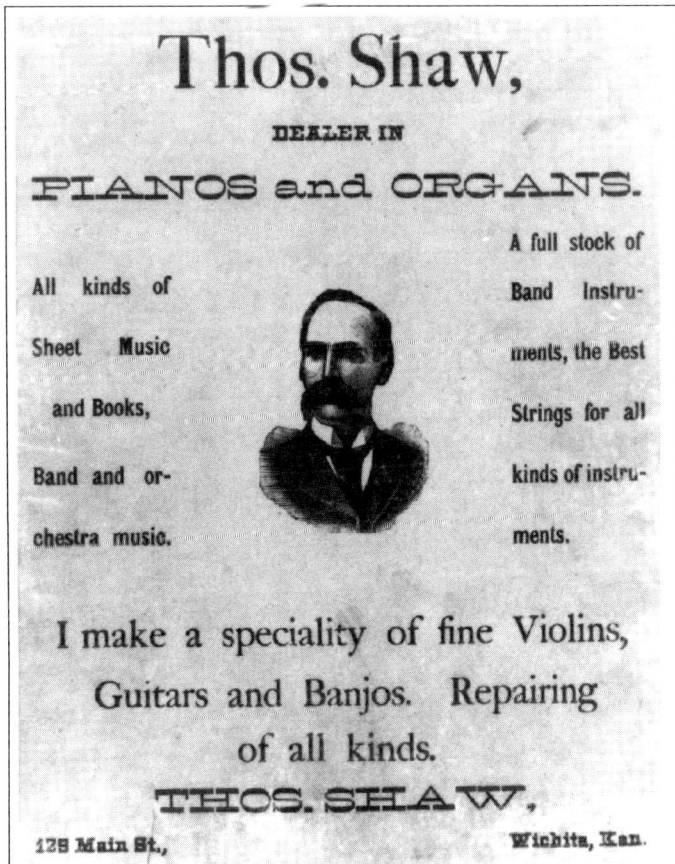

An ad printed on the back of a bound volume of sheet music published by Thomas Shaw, c. 1890.

At the formal opening of the Garfield Opera House on January 25, 1887, Shaw's orchestra played for a comic opera by Robert McCaire adapted to the music from Jacobornski's *Ermine.*

On June 2, 1892, when J. R. Mead's daughter, Mamie, was married at the family home, "Shaw's orchestra furnished the music, and at 7:30 o'clock the soft sweet strains of Mendelssohn's wedding march floated through the room, and to this music the wedding party entered."

Outdoor concerts were popular during the summertime, and in August, 1893, the Sunday School class of the First M.E. Church entertained with a lawn social at which "Ice cream and cake were served from tables by the young ladies, and Shaw's orchestra furnished most excellent music. This is the most charming way of summer evening entertainment."

Shaw's own store was frequently the site of concerts to which he invited the public: "Come in evenings and hear a concert on the cécilium from 7 to 9 o'clock and get a book of old songs free. ... I will entertain you every evening with good music on the various instruments, such as Graphaphone, Orpheus and Apollo, together with my full orchestra."

In addition to music, Thomas Shaw was widely known for the annual Thanksgiving dinners he gave for Wichita's newspaper boys. His wife, Minnie, took pride in her work with the less fortunate, and she looked forward every year to helping the newsboys forget their sorrows for a day. In 1905, the 16th anniversary of the annual dinner, nearly 100 newsboys met at the store for music and speeches, and then marched to the beat of a bass drum over to the Baltimore Hotel (northeast corner of Second and Main)[1] for a "sumptuous repast." After dinner, the boys were treated to a vaudeville performance at the Lyric Theater.

"The Music Man" and dean of music dealers died of pneumonia on October 7, 1913, at the age of 69. His obituary stated: "In addition to conducting the oldest music house, he was head of the oldest firm that had been continuously in business on Main Street or Douglas Avenue for more than a quarter of a century." Thomas Shaw is buried at Wichita's historic Maple Grove Cemetery[2].

---

[1] originally, the Occidental Hotel, as it is also known today
[2] northeast corner of Ninth and Hillside

Note: Unattributed quotations in this article appeared in editions of the Wichita *Eagle* and the Wichita *Beacon* between 1884 and 1913.

"The grandest, biggest, brightest and best excursion that ever left Wichita will leave the Atchison, Topeka and Santa Fe depot Thursday morning, August 6th, at 8 o'clock a.m. for Arkansas City," reported the Wichita *Eagle* in 1885. Rail excursions were very popular during the last half of the 19th century. But this one, claimed supporters, was no ordinary tour: In addition to a train trip and picnic lunch, the outing would include a cruise on the Arkansas River aboard the elegant steamboat *Kansas Miller*[1].

The low fare of $2.00 for adults and $1.00 for the children made the excursion an exceptional value. Seldom had a person been offered so much as this excursion furnished for such a small cost, advertisers urged: "Take your wife and children and set apart August 6th to give them a nice ride on the railroad of 120 miles, a day in the shady grove and a steamboat trip on the Great Arkansas."

Grand Railroad Excursion Included Steamboat Jaunt

The tour was promoted by J. P. Allen, J. M. Balderston, Frank Dale, S. D. Hollowell, William Innes, M. W. Levy, N. F. Niederlander, W. E. Stanley, Fred Sweet, and Sam Woolard — all Wichita leaders. They believed ample preparations had been made for the trip and that it would be a rare treat for excursionists. In the words of J. M. Balderston: "I can't resist taking my whole family. A steamboat ride will be a greater treat for the children than a circus."

J. P. Allen agreed, saying: "A railroad ride, a steamboat ride and a picnic, all in one day, ought to enable a man to forget business and be happy for a whole week."

About half an hour before departure time, a large crowd awaited the arrival of the four coaches and baggage car. So many people had purchased tickets that there was not enough room for everyone to sit in the coaches, so passengers piled on the engine, on the ladder, and on top of the coaches. The lively musical band was the last group to board the train, which departed the depot at 8:30 a.m.

"D. D. Myers, one of the oldest and most popular conductors on the Santa Fe, had charge of the train by special request of the excursionists, who telegraphed the company several days ago that they wanted Myers to run the train."

The morning was bright and cool, and the open windows let in the fresh breeze and the smell of freshly mown hay and ricks of oats. The train sped through Derby, Mulvane, and then stopped at Udall, where a photographer took a picture of the train to sell to passengers along the way.

Continuing through Cowley County along the banks of the Walnut River, the train passed Winfield and arrived at Arkansas City about 10:30 a.m. As the train passed a steep hill in Arkansas City, the engine blew for all to view the "Queen of the Border in the delta of the Arkansas and the Walnut. The train passed on by the depot and down to the road crossing that leads to the Walnut bridge."

Atchison, Topeka & Santa Fe passenger train, c. 1884.

Conveyances were waiting to take the excursionists to the grove on the Walnut River, about half a mile away. Following the musical band down to the river, they picnicked in the grove and then boarded the *Kansas Miller* for the 12-mile trip down the Walnut to the junction of the Arkansas River and return.

At 3:00 p.m., a game of baseball was played in the grove by Arkansas City and Wichita. The Wichita team won 37 to 5 and took the purse of $50, which was raised by the spectators. After the game, the excursionists were taken into town so they could enjoy a meal before returning home. Most had dinner at the Leland Hotel, which "sets a good table, has clean rooms, accommodating servants, and is, as it purports to be, a first-class house."

At 7:00 p.m., the crowd scrambled for seats on the train bound for Wichita, which arrived at the depot at 9:30 p.m. The excursion was, for the most part, a success. There was no water supply on the return trip, however, and some people were disappointed because more tickets were sold than the train could accommodate.

---

[1] a 25-foot x 140-foot stern wheeler weighing approximately 200 tons and able to carry 125 passengers

Note: Unattributed quotations in this article appeared in 1885 issues of the Wichita *Eagle* and the Wichita *Beacon*.

In 1885, Citizens Urged to Be Thankful for Wichita

By 1885, Wichita had come a long way since the day in 1870 when the town was incorporated. It was experiencing the boom of the 1880s, and the population had reached over 17,000. The city had three railroads, about five miles of street railroad, an iron bridge that spanned the river, elevators, mills, iron foundries, and at least ten churches – all things which contributed towards making Wichita a prosperous city.

On Thanksgiving morning, 1885, union church services were held at the First Baptist Church (northeast corner of First and Market Streets). The speaker was the Reverend J. H. Parker, new pastor of the Congregational Church. His text was *Acts 21:39 (a citizen of no mean city)*, and his message for Thanksgiving Day was entitled "The Past, Present and Future of Wichita."

The Reverend himself was a victim of Kansas fever, having only been in Wichita two months. He spoke of the town's early days — its newspapers, banks, and churches. He talked excitedly about the growth Wichita was experiencing and the opportunities that were here. And, he boasted of the Southwest Business College, soon to be the best-equipped commercial college this side of Chicago.

The local newspapers carried most of the Reverend Parker's message:

> I do not believe there is a city in our whole domain that has greater possibilities or better probabilities than our Wichita.... I feel thankful this morning that I have become a citizen of such a thriving city. No place in our republic is better advertised in the east and north. ...The clergy and other Christian workers need the stimulus of these facts, that we may put forth efforts commensurate with the city's importance and needs for her educational, moral and religious interests.... As we look back upon past Wichita in the years to come, and recount anew her glorious progress, it will be a pleasure to say, "I was there"; and we have aided every present and future resident to say honestly and heartily, "I am a citizen of no mean city."... The future citizens of Wichita are to have great advantages and greater responsibilities.

The Reverend said he felt this topic important because "the church interests must keep abreast of the business interests."

One of those business interests was the newly completed Manhattan Hotel (northeast corner of Douglas and Topeka), which had opened in June. The Wichita *Eagle* reported: "The Manhattan has seventy guest rooms.... Its parlors and reception rooms are furnished with a taste and extravagant luxury that is equal to the best houses of the eastern cities."

On Thanksgiving night, the new Manhattan was the scene of a large social gathering, which the papers described in glowing terms: "All who saw the array of beauty, elegance and refinement pronounced it the crowning affair of the most gorgeous of our entertainments. Without enumerating the gentlemen present, it is only necessary to say that they were the representative men of our city, of whom many were from the foremost ranks of the commercial and property circles."

Arnold's Orchestra played superbly as the gentlemen and their ladies danced the evening away. In the parlor could be heard vocal and instrumental numbers performed by various singers and musicians. According to the Wichita *Beacon*, "Mr. Will Collins and Mr. Alden sang a number of songs in a style worthy of professionals, which were greeted with hearty applause." And, in the dining room, the most sumptuous repast, with a bill of fare unequaled and unexcelled, was spread for the refreshment of the invited guests.

The ladies chose the occasion to wear their loveliest costumes, which were described in detail in the local society columns:

> Mrs. L. W. Levy, elaborate black satin en train with jet lace sleeves, diamond ornaments, and scarlet satin petticoat.... Miss Sadie York, ruby satin gown with Spanish lace short sleeves – very stylish.... Miss Lucie Lattck, an elaborate costume of pale blue silk, made en train.... Miss Ida Skinner, very elaborate wine velvet, blue silk front.... Mrs. Harry Peck, ivory satin and brocade, Spanish lace, and diamonds.... Mrs. A. W. Davis, cream lace dress, natural flowers.... Mrs. Charles Smyth, stylish costume of black velvet with jet trimmings, diamonds, and natural flowers.... Mrs. Lindermuth, cream satin bridal dress.... Mrs. Josie Stanley, pink satin with white lace trimming

A special guest of the hotel that evening was Mr. Frank Howard, a traveling correspondent for the Chicago *Inter-Ocean*. No doubt he boasted of the event in his paper.

Time and progress have moved beyond that elegant evening at the Manhattan Hotel on Thanksgiving night in 1885. A poem written for the *Eagle* and published that same Thanksgiving Day is a reminder that, although times have changed, the past still tugs at the heart, especially at such a holiday.

A postcard promoting the Manhattan Hotel, made in Germany and published by Orr's Bookstore in Wichita; the one shown here was mailed in 1909 (Tihen Collection).

Note: Unattributed quotations in this article appeared in the Thanksgiving 1885 issues of the Wichita *Eagle* and the Wichita *Beacon*.

A Thanksgiving Song
by W. H. Tucker

*Of all good things that e're was made,
Or mixed up, wet or dry,
That knocks all others in the shade,
Is grandma's pumpkin pie.*

*It makes you feel so stout an strong,
And grow an inch more high,
To eat a slice both wide and long,
Of grandma's pumpkin pie.*

*No apple dumplins and sweet cream,
Upon your plate piled high —
Can make your life so sweet a dream
As grandma's pumpkin pie.*

*No chicken fixings, cold or hot,
Or beef steak, on the fry,
Nor smashed potatoes in the pot
Like grandma's pumpkin pie.*

*Old grandpa on Thanksgiving day,
With pleasure in his eye,
"Dear children, take a chunk," will say,
"Of Grandma's pumpkin pie."*

*And grandma, dressed in her black silk,
Will say, as she goes by,
"Dear children, sup a glass of milk
With grandma's pumpkin pie."*

[Wichita, Kan., Nov. 1885.]

Master Architect U. G. Charles Set His Sights on Wichita

What do Wichita landmarks Park Villa (North Riverside Park), the Mentholatum Building (northeast corner of Douglas and Cleveland), the Lawrence Block (southeast corner of Douglas and Emporia), and the Hypatia House (1215 North Broadway)[1] have in common? They were all designed by prominent Wichita architect Ulysses Grant Charles.

In the book *Kansas and Kansans,* the following was said of Mr. Charles:

> Of the masters of this art who have contributed much to the past of Wichita, and who, because of their superior equipment and talents, may be counted upon to share in the development of the future of the city, more than passing mention is due U. G. Charles, than whom there is to be found no more talented man in the profession in the state.
>
> Recognized and acknowledged as an expert and authority in his profession, Mr. Charles has been called frequently into court to give expert opinions along lines of mechanical engineering and structural work in the settlement of court matters. His contributions to various magazines and periodicals on technical subjects have been of the greatest value to the profession, and for about two years he was the publisher of a monthly architectural magazine at Wichita which attracted great interest among architects everywhere.

Ulysses Grant Charles was born March 10, 1865, near Salem, Indiana. He served a long apprenticeship in the trades of cabinet maker and general mechanic in two of the leading passenger coach works of the United States. The jobs he performed in those capacities demanded precision craftsmanship.

In 1886, Charles came to Wichita to take advantage of the boom. He worked as a carpenter, carver, and cabinet maker, but when the bust came along a few years later, he began eyeing other opportunities. In 1891, he accepted the position of master mechanic in charge of the design department for the Northwestern Car and Machine Works in Oshkosh, Wisconsin. He also began his architectural career in Wisconsin, working for the Morgan Company, one of the largest manufacturers of sashes, doors, blinds, and interior woodwork in the United States.

Because of his love for Wichita, U. G. Charles returned to the city in 1901 and resumed his architectural career. By then, the bust was over. Wichita was starting to recover financially, and many building projects were beginning to be developed. He soon became well known and one of the most sought-after architects in the midwest.

Charles advertised extensively in city directories, the newspapers, and promotional brochures. Two ads from the 1907 city directory read:

> I make Houses to Fit People
> Some try to Fit People to Houses.
> Which treatment do YOU think is easiest to take?

> Your Minister cares for your soul,
> Your Doctor for your body, Your Lawyer for your property,
> and your Architect makes the Home Convenient and Artistic.

A few years later, ads like the following, taken from the 1914 city directory, were typical:

> See Architect U. G. CHARLES. Why do the citizens of Wichita go to architects located in other parts of the country to make plans for their skyscrapers and best residences? Now Listen. It is for the same reason that other localities call on U. G. CHARLES for their skyscrapers and best residences. Also that U. G. CHARLES has planned and supervised from 75 to 100 buildings in Wichita alone ... and all I require when entering a contract for plans is that the building contract must be let to a RESPONSIBLE AND QUALIFIED CONTRACTOR.

In 1907, the Wichita *Eagle* reported that Charles had received from Pennsylvania a new, $200 "... Wagonhorst electric blue print machine. This is the first machine of this kind west of Kansas City and will make a blue print 48 x 60

This portrait of Ulysses Grant Charles appeared in a 1909 advertisement in the Kansas Farmer's Star.

inches in size. The machine has a large glass drum behind which an adjustable arc light of 2,000 candle power is suspended. With this machine, blue prints can be made in cloudy weather. Heretofore no printing could be done except in the sunlight."

With offices in the Winne Building and, later, in the Schweiter Building, Charles supervised the construction of numerous buildings in Kansas towns like Anthony, Augusta, Caldwell, Conway Springs, Newton, Sedan, Wellington, and Whitewater and in such Oklahoma communities as Blackwell, Tonkawa, and Woodward.

Examples of his work in Wichita include the residences of C. Q. Chandler at 206 Clifton, F. G. Smyth at 1244 North Topeka, C. G. Van Arsdale at 1515 Park Place, H. Van Arsdale at 535 South Fern, James Allison at 1227 University, R. H. Lockwood at 1339 North Lawrence[2], Dr. John L. Evans at 1054 North Lawrence, George Theis at 1031 North Emporia, F. A. Amsden at 1230 North Lawrence, J. H. Meeker at 1427 Park Place, R. P. Murdock at 1602 Park Place, and Otto Weiss at 1045 North Emporia.

Among the buildings designed by Charles were the Fred Farmer Building at 903 West Douglas, the addition to West Side Presbyterian Church, the Odd Fellows Lodge on the southwest corner of 18th Street and Lawrence, the Salvation Army Barracks, and the Metz Lumber Company, Hockaday Paint Company, Brooks Tire Machine Company, and Western Biscuit Company buildings.

One of the architect's most famous designs was neither a residence nor a business, but a 1912 street-lighting project called the "White Way Lights." Suspended from the top of 23-foot poles, which also supported the overhead trolley wires, these ornamental electric lamps served to light up Douglas Avenue.

In 1923, U. G. Charles became a patent attorney. For about six years, he had an office in Topeka. In 1929, he returned to Wichita and shared an office in the Brown Building with his son, Merlin, who took over the architectural business. According to Charles, the United States Patent Office was issuing patents at the rate of 1,000 per week that year.

U. G. Charles remained in Wichita until the last year of his life. He died in Pawnee Rock, Kansas, in 1947, and is buried here in Wichita in the Maple Grove Abbey at Maple Grove Cemetery[3].

---

[1] originally the John H. Butts home
[2] now Broadway
[3] northeast corner of Ninth and Hillside

Horses Were "One of the Family" a Hundred Years Ago

During the twentieth century, transportation has advanced to the point where automobiles, trucks, busses and such have long been taken for granted. In an earlier era, however, horses were "it." So necessary were they for hauling and transporting, horses were viewed as prized possessions. Also looked upon as respected family members, horses were included alongside people in the society columns of newspapers, and their obituaries were frequently noted.

Horses were often named for a close friend of their owner's. William Greiffenstein ("the Father of Wichita") named his trotting horse *Colonel M* in honor of his friend Col. Marshall Murdock, founder and editor of the Wichita *Eagle*. At a race in El Dorado, Kansas, in 1883, *Colonel M* placed second and won $250. When he died in 1884, *Colonel M's* obituary included the fact that Greiffenstein had once refused an offer of $3,000 for him.

At one time, Col. H. G. Toler, owner of the Toler Auditorium, had a large stock farm five miles north of town. About the farm, it was said: "From here have gone some of the world's famous horses." In 1888, the Toler Stock Farm sold a ten-month-old colt named *Red Hood* to the Sherwood and Rohrer Stock Farm of Valley Center for $500. In 1895, they advertised three horses for sale in the *Horse Review*. Within 48 hours after the press was released, two horses were sold, and within one week the other one was sold. As the horse was put on a car to be shipped out, a cablegram was received from a gentleman in England wanting the same horse.

Patchen May Wilkes, a horse belonging to dry goods dealer Cash Henderson, was trained by William King, one of the best-known horse trainers in Kansas. King was the original trainer in Wichita, having settled west of town in the year 1870, and he became renowned for his training of this particular horse. *Patchen May Wilkes* died in 1906.

Pat Reese was the horse of J. F. Reese, cattle dealer and proprietor of the Oriental Stables. In 1898, the Wichita *Eagle* reported: "Pat Reese, the oldest and probably the most prominent carriage horse in Wichita, died yesterday morning. He was about 26 years of age. He has been in the family of J. F. Reese since 1877.... Pat was known to everybody in town, being pitch black, except for a white face and a white left hind foot. He was up to the last very proud in his gait. He saw more of the pomp of parade than any other horse in Wichita, for everybody wanted to borrow him to ride in the procession...."

In 1908, *Old Jack*, a large draft horse for Maple Grove Cemetery, died. He had worked at the cemetery 18 years and was 26 years old. "The cemetery officials say he will be hard to replace as he was an intelligent animal and knew his work well."

Little Brownie was the well-known horse that pulled the stage from Emporia to Wichita. William C. Little, Probate Judge of Sedgwick County, came to Wichita in 1870 as a passenger on *Little Brownie's* stage.

Pat Arnold was the horse belonging to C. C. Arnold, a veterinary surgeon and one of the earliest settlers of Sedgwick County. Arnold was noted for his kindness and compassion to horses. When his own *Pat* died, he commented that he wished to be buried next to him some day.

Col. Marshall Murdock drove a sulky drawn by a daughter of *Pat Arnold's*. Murdock's brother, Roland P., was a horse financier and owned the fast-pacing *Wichita Charley*.

In its earlier days, Wichita was famous for the breeding of fine horses, and leading horsemen from all over the country came to the horse sales here. In March of 1893, the *Eagle* announced a breeders' sale of trotting stock and referred to Wichita as "the Lexington of the west." Among the dignitaries who came to the sale was Chicagoan Will Logan, Jr., of *Clark's Horse Journal*.

Photo of William Greiffenstein, c. 1878.

In 1889, a local newspaper told of a four-year-old boy who, while standing near his papa, was kicked by the family horse. "The little fellow got up after taking a survey of the situation, looked up in his father's face and said, 'Papa, guess Tom kicked me because he thought I was a Democrat.'"

Lizzie Mathewson, wife of "Buffalo Bill" Mathewson, enjoyed riding her favorite mare, *Bess*, who could "outrun anything in the country."

When Archibald L. Derby, pioneer oilman and founder of the Derby Oil Company, died in Wichita in 1956, the New York *Times* stated that he was "owner and breeder of many harness race horses, the best known being Yankee Main, winner of the 1944 Hambletonian at Goshen, New York."

In 1887, Sam Hewey, proprietor of the Topeka Avenue Livery Stable, invited the editor of a local newspaper, the *Sunday Growler,* to visit his stables. He was boarding over 50 horses at the time and stated that Wichita "owns more fine horses than any city of double its size I have ever been in." He showed the newspaper man several horses: *Jack,* one of the most stylish horses in the state, owned by A. L. Houck; *Barney Wilkes,* the best livery horse in the West; and *Elder,* valued at $500 and worth every dollar, owned by the Reverend J. B. Hewitt.

Photo of a horse identified as one of Greiffenstein's, c. 1885.

Hewey also stocked all varieties and makes of carriages and hacks and was prepared at all times to furnish conveyances to ladies for shopping, calling, and pleasure trips. He was also prepared at all times to fill orders for choice roadsters direct from their noted stock farm in Kentucky.

Early Wichitans were proud to go riding around the city with their prized horse. All they needed to go with it was a fancy carriage; and, as early as 1873, Packer's Stables was advertising "Packer's new easy riding, Pullman palace family carriage."

Note: Unattributed quotations in this article appeared in write-ups published in the Wichita *Eagle* and the Wichita *Beacon* between 1873 and 1908.

In Spite of Recent Bust, Christmas Spirit Boomed in 1896

The holiday season is a time for reminiscing – reflecting upon occasions when the family was together, recalling a favorite Christmas program at church or school, or remembering a unique downtown Christmas scene. Christmastime in Wichita in the year 1896 provides just such a juncture.

Hints that the economy was still not good were contained in articles like the one that appeared in the Wichita *Daily Eagle* on December 24: "…yesterday was the best business day for the purchase of Christmas goods. …Where do the people get the money from? That is a puzzle to everybody. A week ago everybody was complaining of a scarcity of funds, and now the people seem to have lots of it. …The lively trade indicates one thing or another. The people either have more money than they pretend they have or else they beat the world in loving their children. Christmas toys are seen going in every direction."

Indeed, to hear the merchants talk, it was business as usual. The Boston Store advertised that they were "the greatest distributors of Holiday goods in Kansas." To meet the demand, the store had hired "10 extra wrappers, 10 extra cash boys and 50 extra salespeople to attend to your wants." Santa Claus was on hand to greet the little ones and find out what they wanted for Christmas. Bulky toys like wagons, hobby horses, and sleighs were displayed outside.

Downtown store windows were sights to behold, as merchants went all out to attract Christmas shoppers. One of the best window displays was that of the Bitting Bros. store, which depicted Santa Claus seated in a sleigh being drawn by an elk through a snow storm. Cotton batting was used for the snow, and the display represented "a truly Icelandic scene."

The children especially seemed to enjoy the window of the A. N. Kellogg Newspaper Company, which was outlined in holly and mistletoe, framing a lifelike nature scene. In the center, a bare oak tree served as a playground for five frisky squirrels and a beautiful pair of Kansas' favorite red birds. A covey of quail joined English sparrows and a feeding pigeon in the foreground; a large grey eagle with a quail clutched in his talons soared overhead; and a screech owl could be seen in the background. At one end was a miniature lake with a duck ready to fly from the attack of a wildcat, which was trying to secure it for a Christmas feast. "The birds were all killed in Sedgwick County by Gerald Volk, and the taxidermist was Mrs. Volk."

Photo of the Bitting Bros. Department Store, c. 1880.

Cash Henderson's window displayed an electric fountain – "a thing of beauty" – which attracted much attention along with a great deal of speculation concerning how it worked.

Among the antiques in The Model's unusual window display were a newspaper published at Kingston, Virginia, on January 4, 1800, containing news of George Washington's death; a 100-year-old rifle; and a copy of the marriage license of Abraham Lincoln and Mary Todd. And, of course, there was Santa Claus with his smile and happy expression.

Erp and Wickersham's Shoe Store chose the theme of "Santa Claus Up to Date" for their holiday window, which presented Santa mounted upon a bicycle carrying his pack upon his back.

On Christmas Day, the paper commented on the brisk holiday trade: "The crowds did not disappear until nearly midnight last night. This morning as old sol advances his golden circle from the Atlantic across to the Pacific, he awakens the happy children as he goes, to enjoy the happiest day to them in all the year, and the old motto expresses the sentiment of the day better than anything else: 'Peace on earth, good will toward men.' "

As in other years, businesses, charitable groups, and civic clubs saw to it that the city's underprivileged children had a Christmas celebration. The youngsters at the Children's Home enjoyed a Christmas tree, gifts donated by merchants, and a visit from Santa Claus. The Salvation Army treated some 200 children to Christmas dinner, while the First Presbyterian

Church distributed gifts to the poor on Christmas Eve.

Children at the Masonic Home were given a surprise Christmas party planned by the ladies of the Eastern Star and financed by contributions from the Masonic bodies. When all the expected guests arrived, everyone assembled on the third floor, where a Christmas tree had been decorated and gifts were presented to each child. The children, in turn, surprised the guests with a musical program consisting of songs and recitations they had planned to give to the Matron of the home.

Following tradition, Christmas programs were held in churches throughout the city. The First Presbyterian Church gave a program entitled "The Preparation For, and the Coming of Santa Claus." Afterwards, bags of candy were passed out.

The First Baptist Sunday School presented a cantata, *Santa Claus and Mother Goose*, in which all the characters were dressed in costume. At the end of the program, everyone was given an artistic Christmas card as a souvenir and a bag containing candy, nuts, and popcorn.

At the Cathedral, the choir and soloist Mrs. Catherine Russell, accompanied by the "master hand" of Clarence Eddy at the organ, presented *Laudati*.

Those attending the Christmas Eve service at the Lincoln Street Presbyterian Church were probably among the most thankful Wichitans that night. The Sunday School program centered around a Christmas tree, which was decorated with cotton and loaded with toys. At the moment when the candles on the tree were to be lit, one candle was insecurely fastened in the small tin socket which held it; and, after being lit, "it fell out of its place to the floor, the blaze still burning as it dropped. The cotton and light inflammable material caught at once at the bottom of the tree. … In an instant, the blaze rushed to the top-most twig, and the entire tree was one brilliant mass of flame." Luckily, Mrs. Richard Hathaway was able to stop the fire, and the program resumed with no real harm done.

Most Wichitans greeted Christmastime 1896 with thankful hearts, and the poem written by Wichitan J.S. Jennings for the *Eagle* and published on Christmas Day probably expressed the people's sentiments.

The Gift of Victory

Take care of yourself. Your Father gave
His own dear Son yourself to save.
Take care of others and you will do
As you would have others do unto you.

Give unto others. Nothing to give?
He gave His life that you might live.
Give Him your love – give Him a lift,
For eternal life was a Christmas gift.

Nothing to give? Give Him your love;
Your will is the deed to mansions above.
Your will may be all you have to give
"Look up to Him, and you shall live."

Good will on earth is peace begun;
Good will is worth the victory won.
Good will is worth your Father's care –
A Son on earth, in Heaven an heir.

With His kind care your troubles cease,
For He giveth His beloved – His beloved peace.
"Glory in the highest" will triumph then,
With "peace on earth, good will to men."

Note: Unattributed quotations in this article appeared in the Christmas 1896 issues of the Wichita *Eagle* and the Wichita *Beacon*.

First *Messiah* Production a Crowning Achievement

Wichita's Auditorium (southwest corner of First and St. Francis)[1] was filled to capacity for the city's first rendition of Handel's *Messiah*, which was performed two days after Easter, on April 12, 1898. Over 600 people from Wellington, Winfield, Hutchinson, El Dorado, Newton, and as far away as Guthrie and Oklahoma City, came to Wichita on special trains. It was the largest attendance up to that time for an event where admission was charged. Reserved seats under the balcony were 50 cents; on first floor, 75 cents; in the balcony, $1.00.

Large, half-page advertisements promoting the concert appeared in the Wichita *Eagle*: "WICHITA'S GREATEST MUSICAL EVENT…'The Messiah' Chorus is the largest and best-trained of any ever having appeared in Wichita … Every soloist an artist."

Produced locally under the auspices of the Wichita Musical Club and directed by Miss Jessie Clark, the *Messiah* featured renowned guest soloists and a chorus of 133 voices. Accompaniment was provided by Gertie Calhoun, pianist; Mrs. D. W. Pitts, organist; and the Thomas Shaw Orchestra.

Guest artists included Mabel Clare-Larimer, who had charmed Wichita before with her clear, pure-toned, contralto voice; Lester Bartlett Jones, tenor, a professor of elocution at Ottawa University and a graduate of Knox College Conservatory of Music; and Harry C. McClung, who had appeared in Wichita before and was called "Wichita's favorite baritone" in a Wichita *Eagle* review.

Madame Genevra Johnstone-Bishop, one of America's greatest oratorio singers, was supposed to take the soprano role. At the last minute, however, she became ill and could not attend. Helen Buckley was found as a replacement. Miss Buckley, from London, was currently singing in Chicago and receiving the highest salary paid to a singer in a church at that time. She had appeared in the *Messiah* back in Handel's old stomping ground and was familiar with the role. So, what threatened to be a calamity turned out to be an undisguised blessing.

The Wichita production was a financial success, thanks to business managers O. A. Boyle and Walter A. Vincent. In a review of the event, the Wichita *Eagle* reported with pride:

> Those present will long remember the panoramic spectacle that appealed to the eye when cast upon that magnificent audience of the best and most intelligent people of this section, gathered from this and surrounding towns. Three thousand people such as these are not often got together. … Not alone has the uncouth and mediocre west been successful in raising corn and engineering real estate booms, but as well in the realms of the grand art of finished music have talents and rare ability been demonstrated.

Photo of the Toler Auditorium, corner of First Street and St. Francis, c. 1880.

But not all of Wichita's talent was aimed at music that Easter. Wichitan Harriet Loretta Knapp wrote the following poem for the Wichita *Mirror*, which reaches the sentiment across the ages:

A Dream of Easter Morn

Lilies, lilies everywhere;
Easter lilies, sweet and fair;
So pure and white, So tender bright,
Blooming, blooming everywhere!

Cherubs, cherubs everywhere!
Little cherubs sweet and fair,
In gauzy white, On pinions light,
Flying, flying everywhere!

Singing, singing everywhere!
Upon the music laden air,
The rich perfume, Of each white bloom
Like incense rises everywhere.

Winging, winging everywhere;
In maizy whirl, Oh picture rare!
The lilies smile, And would beguile
These cherubs flitting everywhere.

Each cherub plucks a lily white;
Then spreads its wings in noiseless flight
Till all are gone, But still the song
Is echoing through the perfumed air
"Tis Easter morn! Tis Easter morn!
The risen Christ reigns everywhere."

---

[1] owned for several years by actor Sidney Toler's family and known as the Toler Auditorium

In 1899, downtown Wichita was the very heart of "southwestern" Kansas. One week in October, the railroads alone brought 42,000 extra passengers to town. Crowds poured into the city from every direction, and in the space of six days, the local economy had been enriched by more than $700,000. What attracted so many visitors to Wichita that week? The city's first street fair and carnival, held October 16-21. According to an estimate in the Wichita *Beacon*, "185,000 people went through the street fair arch."

The extravaganza was widely promoted by colored lithographs advertising the carnival and its many attractions – like Iterbo, the sensational European high-wire bicyclist, and world-renowned aeronauts Baldwin and Carrow, who made daily balloon ascensions near the Sedgwick County Courthouse.

Souvenir buttons in four different designs were sold for ten cents each. One showed the corner of Main and Douglas; another depicted the street fair entrance. A third

1899 Street Fair and Carnival Set a Tradition in Motion

bore the message: "Just tell them that you saw me at the Wichita street fair." The fourth and most popular button featured two carnival figures holding an ear of corn, with the official title and date of the fair printed in black letters around the edge of the button.

The opening events included three parades: the Carnival Parade, which boasted masqueraders, bands, and skyrockets; the Civic Parade, composed of 75 decorated merchant floats and 12 fairy floats built by Tomey & Co. of the Olympic Theater in St. Louis, Missouri; and the Flower Parade, described as "a dream of beauty" with its beautiful carriages and Miss Mayme Mahaney, the carnival queen. Queen Mayme was tendered a waltz song, *My Own, My Queen*, written by Mrs. R. E. Guthrie and arranged by Prof. C. H. Blume.

The carnival site encompassed a square block beginning at the City Building¹, extending south on Main to English, east on English to Market, then north on Market to William. Crowds entered the carnival through a beautifully decorated archway on Main Street just south of William. Incandescent lamps covered the face of the arch, and when lighted, the effect was dazzling. Both the large star placed upon the top of the arch and the globe in the center were illuminated with colored lights, which were also used to outline the upper edge of the arch. The splendor of the arch could best be appreciated when seen at night.

Just inside the entrance was "King Corn," a striking exhibit and most elaborate structure, which had been set up by the Santa Fe railroad. The figure of

One of four different souvenir buttons promoting the 1899 Street Fair and Carnival (Tihen Collection).

King Corn sat on a massive throne which surmounted a pavillion; the tip of his crown measured 32 feet off the ground. Purple-colored corn husks formed the body, kernels of corn covered the face and hands, and corn silk served as the hair and beard. On the four walls of the ground floor of the pavillion were inscriptions that read, respectively:

> Kansas leads all the corn states.
> The biggest crop of corn ever raised in Kansas.
> Kansas harvests one-sixth of the United States corn crop.
> Kansas wears the champion corn belt.

The second floor of the pavillion was a bandstand — a remarkable piece of work that came from Emporia, Kansas.

Midway attractions included Hagenback's Wild Animal Show, Streets of Cairo, Turkish Theater, Japanese Theater, Temple of Isis Theater, Palace of Varieties, and Moving Pictures.

Among the many booths (which were covered with t~~ ~~aper in such an attractive way as to not look like temporary displays) was the outstanding exhibit of the Missouri ar~~ ~~ansas Telephone Company, which showed a switchboard and the long-distance phone with the new speaking tube in a sound-proof booth. Visitors could listen to music through the receivers provided.

The Wichita Trunk Factory booth displayed the new "Hossfeld Chiffonier Trunk" by Wichita inventor, William Hossfeld, brother of the proprietor. At one end of the booth, a workman explained the process of trunk-making to visitors.

Nearly every musical instrument imaginable could be seen at the Thomas Shaw Music Store booth. There was a concert every evening, and sheet music was given away as a souvenir.

Items for sale at John McComb's Harness and Saddlery Shop were attractively displayed in a booth outfitted with handsome plush robes on the walls and carpet on the floor to show off the saddles, harnesses, and harness supplies.

Visitors felt like they had been transported to Japan when they arrived at the George Innes Dry Goods booth and saw the richly colored rugs.

The Ascetylene Gas Company booth was constructed to represent a parlor scene in an old castle. The area was brilliantly lighted with ascetylene gas, which was manufactured by a machine as visitors watched.

City schools were dismissed at 1:00 p.m. Monday through Thursday, but all day on Friday so that boys and girls could attend "Children's Day" at the fair. In honor of the occasion, the Jacob Dold Packing Company provided a free lunch for the children at its booth, which resembled an up-to-date beef and pork establishment.

State officials attending the fair boasted that it was the greatest event in Kansas. As Governor Stanley put it, "I am proud of the success Wichita is making of its street fair. I tell you gentlemen, this is the best city on earth."

The *Beacon* concurred: "The fair reunited everybody in Wichita. The people are more unanimous than ever in the belief that Wichita has wonderful opportunities and that unity will develop it into a great city. In that one respect alone the fair has been worth ten times more than it cost."

As Wichita's first street fair and carnival came to a close, plans were already being made for the next year. In the meantime, King Corn and some other exhibits were put on a special train to Guthrie, Oklahoma, where they were to be loaned for use there at a similar event.

---

[1] which now houses the Wichita-Sedgwick County Historical Museum

Note: Unattributed quotations in this article were taken from October 1899 issues of the Wichita *Eagle* and the Wichita *Beacon*.

The Millers: Educator and Entertainer Extraordinaire

In researching Wichita's past, it is always interesting to run across a husband and wife who both deserve to have their respective stories recorded. Professor Hacke S. Miller and his wife, Nettie, are one such couple.

H. S. and Nettie Miller were married in Sumner County, Kansas, in 1891 and soon afterwards moved to Wichita, where they joined the First Presbyterian Church and became very active in the community. They resided for years at 1331 North Broadway.

Nettie Miller was a nationally known concert whistler and bird imitator. She performed throughout the country and locally, at such places as the Wichita Country Club, the Wichita Forum, and area schools. Wherever she went, praise and recommendations followed.

The Los Angeles *Times* called her a "most brilliant and artistic whistler." And, Yellowstone Park hostess Martha Hopkins stated, "It gives me great pleasure to recommend Mrs. H. S. Miller as a whistler of rare ability. ... I have used some of the finest talent as entertainers for our guests, and I consider Mrs. Miller one of the finest I have heard."

The Kansas State Teachers Association spoke very highly of her, as reported by the Wichita *Eagle*: "There are very few whistlers who attempt anything so ambitious as grand opera arias, yet Mrs. Miller whistles these difficult and lengthy numbers with perfect ease. An authority on the art of whistling declares she is the only woman whistler in America who has a natural warble."

And, according to the Wichita *Beacon*: "Mrs. Miller possesses marked ability as a whistler of ballads and classical numbers. She is showing that whistling can be developed from stage and parlor tolerance to platform art. Mrs. Miller possesses a charming personality and stage presence which add much to her success."

The society columns frequently reported on Mrs. Miller's activities. In September of 1929, she treated her whistling pupils to a bird hike at Sim Park. The early evening was spent observing birds and bird calls, and the outing concluded with a wiener toast. And, on March 20, 1931, the Kansas Whistling Chorus, under Mrs. Miller's direction, presented a benefit concert for the Roosevelt Junior High School P.T.A. The numbers presented by the chorus, the solos by Mrs. Miller, and the finger whistling by Myrtle Hatton of Wellington, Kansas, were rare musical entertainment.

On June 17, 1937, the first Wichita Garden Club meeting of the season was held at the home of Mr. and Mrs. W. B. Millison (1845 Wellington Place) as a memorial to her father, L. W. Clapp, who had recently passed away. It had been a yearly tradition for him to host a Garden Club meeting at the Clapp compound. Over 200 people enjoyed the beautiful lawn and landscaping, the garden and lily pond. It was an ideal place for Mrs. Miller's lecture, "A Trip Through Birdland with Human Birds." She was assisted by the members of her whistling chorus, who scattered out among the trees and shrubs and gave bird calls.

In addition to the Garden Club, Nettie Miller belonged to the Saturday Afternoon Music Club and the Audubon Society. She died in 1957 at the age of 87.

After he and his wife moved to Wichita, H. S. Miller taught at the Southwestern Business College. In 1895, he took a position at a business college in Grand Island, Nebraska. The following year, he opened his first business college in Hastings, Nebraska. At the time, he also had an interest in the Wichita Commercial College. Miller sold his interest in both schools in 1909 and spent the next few years examining various textbooks, course work, and the best business colleges in the West.

On January 3, 1911, Prof. Miller bought out the Wichita Commercial College, renamed it the Miller Business College, and moved it to the sixth floor of the new Butts Building at 145-149 North Lawrence[1]. The brochure for the college said it had first-class elevator service and no steps to climb. Besides halls, closets, and cloak rooms, there was a business practice room, shorthand room, typewriting room, and a fine suite of office rooms. "It is a model place in which to do school work; no dust, flies, no noise from the street, no heat reflection, with excellent light and ventilation. We believe it to be the finest and best-equipped school in the Southwest."

By 1913, Miller advertised his enterprise as The School of Efficiency. Known for its high standards and experienced instructors, the stenotype school included courses in business, penmanship, shorthand, telegraphy, stenotype, and typewriting. In addition, special training was given for Civil Service. In 1917, he sold the business college to Harvey J.

Freeman, its secretary, and the school reverted to the Wichita Commercial College.

Miller then founded Opportunity School, a night school for working people that offered classes in practical subjects such as salesmanship, domestic science, trades, and general education. Courses in mechanical drawing, millinery, and bricklaying were also taught. By 1926, 1,500 people were enrolled in Opportunity School, which had 29 teachers on staff and was located in the high school building[2] at 320-350 North Emporia.

On April 24, 1928, the *Eagle* reported: "H. S. Miller, head of the commercial department of Wichita high school…is a recognized authority on salesmanship and merchandising. He has studied in stores of many cities. The course of lectures embraces salesmanship, leadership, personality and how to develop it, fear and its antidote, mental law of sales, knowing the goods and studying the customers."

H. S. Miller, also known as "High School" Miller, was active in the Kansas State Teachers Association, Wichita Lodge Number 99, the Wichita Consistory, and the Midian Shrine. He died in 1935 at age 72.

---

[1] now Broadway
[2] today, the Wichita Vocational-Technical School

More Glimpses of People from Wichita's Past

Researching Wichita's history in the early newspapers yields bits of information about a number of Wichita citizens, all of whom have contributed to our community.

In 1898, Professor J. C. Marriager, a music teacher, composed a military march entitled *Marching Through Havana*. He was unable to enlist at the time because of wounds he had previously received while serving in the army. So, he did the next best thing and composed a march for the boys, which he asked to be played by the regimental band when the troops invaded Cuba. Marriager dedicated his march to Col. Thomas G. Fitch, who led the 21st Regiment Kansas Volunteer Infantry during the Spanish-American War.

James Allison was a westside developer, instrumental in the founding of Friends University and the man for whom Allison Junior High was named. He was also a first cousin and boyhood playmate of President William McKinley. According to Allison's obituary, which appeared in the Wichita *Eagle* and *Beacon* in November 1916, "In 1900 Mr. Allison was appointed by President McKinley to be one of the United States Commissioners at the Paris Exposition and for six months represented this country in an official capacity abroad."

Dr. W. B. Hendryx, the first president of Garfield University[1], did much to develop the area surrounding the campus into a university community. The school was named after President Garfield, who was the roommate of Dr. Hendryx at Hiram College in Mentor, Ohio. University Avenue was patterned after Euclid Avenue in Cleveland. From these associations came the street names of Hendryx, Hiram, Mentor, and Euclid. Shirley Avenue was named in honor of Dr. Hendryx's son.

After the turn of the century, the father of Orville and Wilbur Wright came to Wichita on several occasions to visit his cousin, Mrs. G. M. Glenn. In 1908, Mrs. Glenn told the Wichita *Beacon:* "The Wright Brothers first rigged up a gliding machine and then both boys would get upon a hill and jump off attempting to glide through the air in their crude machine."

In 1907, actor Sidney Toler came to Wichita with his new bride, Vivian Marston, to visit his family. At one of the parties given in her honor, Mrs. Toler told women how she avoided having to wear warm hosiery: When unable to purchase half-length women's hosiery, she simply asked for small sizes in the men's department. Wichita women liked the idea and told their friends about it. In 1912, when newspapers throughout the United States reported the new fad of women wearing men's silk hose in lieu of their own, Wichita women boasted that the country seemed to be awakening to a good idea that they themselves had known about for several years.

When Woolf Brothers (southwest corner of Market and Douglas) held their grand opening on January 8, 1923, flowers were handed out by special guest Mildred Harris, the former Mrs. Charlie Chaplin. Miss Harris was in Wichita starring in the vaudeville comedy *Movie Mad* at the Orpheum Theater.

George Innes, founder of the Geo. Innes Company, was a good friend of Marshall Field, owner of the famed Chicago emporium. Innes had worked for Field in Chicago, where he was living at the time of the Great Fire of 1871. In 1935, a new shopping train called *The Marshall*

Portrait of George Innes, c. 1880.

Field Merchandise Express was touring the country and stopped in Wichita. At Union Station, the 11-car, air-conditioned "catalog on wheels" was opened to invited retail merchants, who visited luxurious display rooms outfitted with samples of the newest variety of merchandise from the Chicago market. This train was the first ever used for the sale and display of dry goods, apparel, and hardware lines. Walter P. Innes, nephew of George Innes and president of the Geo. Innes Company, was responsible for seeing that it came through Wichita and greeted the train when it pulled into town.

Photo of the Innes Dry Goods store at 123-7 North Main, c. 1900.

---

[1] now Friends University

In 1903, Mayor Proclaimed Observance of Memorial Day

Decoration Day, or "Memorial Day" as it is now known, was originally the day set aside to honor America's Civil War comrades. Today, it not only encompasses veterans from all wars, but also is an occasion to decorate the graves of family and friends.

Although Memorial Day services continue to be held, they are not the same as they used to be. One to be recalled is the ceremony held in Wichita on May 30, 1903. In accordance with the proclamation of President Theodore Roosevelt and Kansas Governor Willis J. Bailey, Wichita Mayor Ben McLean had issued a Memorial Day Proclamation: Employers were to close their businesses, and all citizens were urged to observe the day with

> respect for the dead veterans, both military and naval, of the civil war, commensurate with the standard of American loyalty which they set for us when the unity of our nation was imperiled. ...The valiant work the veterans of the civil war have done for Kansas, in the development of its resources, in the building of its character, and in giving direction to its unique and sturdy civilization, calls for unusual respect from her people, and there is no time more fitting to pay that respect than on the day set apart to honor their dead.

Mayor Ben McLean also reminded the public that there were some veterans still living, and tribute needed to be paid to them. "The day will soon come when we shall better appreciate their usefulness to their country and realize more fully the part they played in making America the greatest nation on earth."

In honor of the occasion, many merchants had decorated their storefront windows. Greenfield Brothers (southwest corner of Market and Douglas) displayed a collection of army paraphernalia and clothing, along with pictures of the war. Across the street, Herman & Hess displayed a white gate guarded by two private soldiers, behind which was a large picture of Abraham Lincoln.

The day was chilly and rainy, and many people were concerned with the high waters from recent heavy rains. But the weather didn't stop others from taking part in the day's activities. The early morning street cars were filled with people carrying bouquets or baskets of flowers on their way to the cemetery.

At the Santa Fe depot, 200 people waited to board the *Frisco's Special*, which was scheduled to take the old soldiers and their auxiliaries to the Highland and Maple Grove Cemeteries at Ninth and Hillside, where ritualistic services were to be held. On hand were the Eggleston Post G.A.R.; its auxiliary, the Caroline Harrison Circle; and about 50 children "bearing boxes and bouquets of flowers and evergreen sprigs." Also participating were the Garfield Post with its auxiliary, the Women's Relief Corps, and the Sons of Veterans (Anson Skinner Camp) along with its auxiliary, the Ladies' Aid Society.

When all had arrived at the depot,

> ...the platform was crowded, and the sprinkling of flowers among the uniforms of blue, and the contrast of youth and beauty of the children with the age and seriousness of the veterans and their wives made the picture a typical one of memorial day. ...The entire body was beautifully decorated with floral tokens that were to be placed on the graves of the remembered dead. The post flags and smaller flags of bright stars and stripes were carried, and their fluttering beauty served to lighten the gloom of the dismal day.

Because of the high water, train No. 309 from St. Louis, due in at 8:15 a.m., was late in arriving. With four coaches fully loaded – the first two with children and decorations, and the last two with posts and auxiliaries – "the train was a vestibule greenhouse at the time it pulled from the station" at 10:20 a.m. Following the services at Highland and Maple Grove, the train returned to the Santa Fe depot, around noon. The cost of the round trip was ten cents per person.

At 2:00 p.m. that day, all G.A.R. posts and their auxiliaries, the Kansas National Guard, the mayor, and city officials met at First and Main to begin the march to the Auditorium. Sanford's Band led the parade and was followed by flower girls wearing red, white, and blue sashes and carrying small flags. The march went south on Main to Douglas, east to St. Francis, and north to First. When they arrived at the hall, it was filled to overflowing.

The meeting was called to order by commander of the Eggleston Post, T. R. Hornaday, and the invocation was given by the Reverend Dr. Bradt of the First Presbyterian Church. Musical numbers included *America*, *Dixie*, and *The Star Spangled Banner*, sung by Misses Parrett and Southwell and accompanied by Mrs. Bruce Griffith, and *Nearer My God to Thee*, performed by Sanford's Band.

Congressman-elect Victor Murdock then "...spoke very feelingly of Memorial Day, of the obligation of citizens to its observance and the commemorating of the brave deeds of the dead heroes of the Civil War. He spoke of the day as being especially impressive and solemn, and said that it should be forever commemorated and honored by the citizens of the republic. The address was received with warm applause."

Murdock's remarks were followed by those of Mrs. Metcalf, wife of Professor Metcalf, who spoke of the martyred president, Abraham Lincoln, and described Lincoln's trip to Gettysburg. After Mrs. Metcalf recited *The Gettysburg Address*, 14-year-old Clara Appling recited *The Boys in Blue* in a masterly manner.

The address for the day was given by Judge S. S. Ashbaugh. He spoke at length about some of the battles fought during the Civil War and concluded by saying: "Unto all those who gave to their country their life's full measure of devotion, regardless of rank or influence, we pay today our heart's respect."

The next day, the papers reported: "Despite the unfavorable weather, the attendance was large, and the exercises, if not the best, were among the best ever witnessed in Wichita. ... Many old soldiers were too feeble to brave the weather, but those who did go were inspired with the thoughts of the brave deeds of those whom they were to honor."

Note: Unattributed quotations in this article appeared in the Memorial Day 1903 issues of the Wichita *Eagle* and the Wichita *Beacon*.

Wichita has experienced several floods over the years, but the worst one by far was the deluge of 1904. Damages were estimated to exceed $200,000. Although the flood of 1877 was also serious, in 1904, a few days after Wichitans had celebrated the Fourth of July, the scene was like it had never been before.

On July 6th, water by the Douglas Avenue Bridge registered eight feet, six inches, and crowds gathered to witness the bathing beach that had been established at the west end of the bridge. Both street car service and train service had ceased. News carriers delivered papers in rowboats, and boats were seen tied to porch steps and gates. A lady lying in a hammock dallied her fingers in the water that lapped at the edge of her front porch. A gentleman sitting in an arm chair on the veranda of his home was smoking a pipe and holding a fishing pole. Boys lying on a flat board paddled around the yard, while toddlers had to be guarded constantly against getting close enough to the water to drown.

1904 Flood Left Devastation in Its Wake

The hardest hit areas included North Riverside Park, the downtown business district, the area surrounding Chisholm Creek, and the fertile farmland lying north of the city between the two rivers and extending on either side, which was completely under water.

North Riverside was one of the first areas to be submerged. All of its drives, flower beds, and benches were under water. On the south side and in the district bordering Riverside and the banks of the Little River, hundreds of homes were submerged. The water in Wichita Street, north of Second Street, was so deep that many small houses were afloat. Just north of Central Avenue, a house had floated up against a larger cottage that stood firmly on its foundation. And, outhouses were everywhere: in the streets, in front yards, lodged against larger buildings, up against front doors.

Downtown, the deepest water was in the area around the Manhattan Hotel at the corner of Topeka and Douglas. Nine inches of water covered the hotel's first floor, which included the office, billiard room, lavatories, barber shop, bar, cigar stand, sample rooms, engine room, and coal house. Guests were not evacuated, however, because the dining room and kitchen were on the second floor, and boats were in service to convey guests to and from the hotel through the flooded district, and to get them to the depots when it was safe to travel again.

North Main as it looked during the 1904 flood.

Damages in the downtown sector alone were estimated to exceed $30,000: $9,875 to Douglas Avenue; $2,775 to Main Street between Central and Douglas Avenue; $2,000 to other downtown streets; $12,500 to the residential district; and $3,000 to miscellaneous property, for a total of $30,150. The primary damage was to fixtures and furnishings: Paint and varnish were defaced, panels warped and cracked, wallpaper peeled off, and linoleum was ruined.

Everybody talked about the flood. It was even the sermon topic at many churches throughout the city, as ministers drew illustrations from the excitement of the week. Since high water had closed some of the other downtown churches, a good-sized crowd was in attendance at St. John's Episcopal[1]. Speaking on the subject "Did God Send It?", the Reverend Dr. J. D.

Ritchey concluded his sermon with the following observation: "It is in such times as this that the great ties of universal brotherhood are seen. Somehow the spirit of God gets into men and the fruit of the Christian spirit is seen."

Several meetings with city officials, the City Council, and the public were held to determine how to prevent another catastrophe. They considered such solutions as widening the channels of both rivers, the removal of Ackerman's Island[2], dredging Chisholm Creek and widening the channel, and the extension of dikes on the Little Arkansas. But, in fact, it was many years before the "Big Ditch" made flood control a reality in Wichita.

---

[1] corner of Third and Topeka
[2] then located in the Arkansas River between Douglas Avenue and Second Street

Note: Unattributed quotations in this article were taken from the Wichita *Beacon* and the Wichita *Eagle's* coverage of the 1904 flood.

Movie Actor Got His Start on Wichita Stage

Sidney Sommers Toler is best remembered for his portrayal of Chinese detective Charlie Chan in the movies. But, his early acting career was also interesting, and little has been written about it.

Sidney's parents, H. G. and Sallie Toler, were prominent members of Wichita society. For several years, they owned the Toler Auditorium on the southwest corner of St. Francis and First Street. Many celebrated entertainers appeared on that stage, but it was also a training ground for local talent, some of whom went on to become famous performers.

Inspired by his mother to become an actor, Sidney made his acting debut in one of her plays, *Tom Sawyer*. Although he left Wichita to pursue a stage career in the East, he returned home periodically to visit family and friends.

His visit to Wichita in the summer of 1907 was one Sidney would always remember. His father had passed away the year before, and he would be acting for the last time on the stage of the family-owned Toler Auditorium. On the brighter side, Sidney was accompanied by his new bride, Vivian Marston, "a vivacious young woman and charming actress, also." A round of parties welcoming the couple to Wichita included two hosted by Mrs. Amos Burns: a whist party, where Mrs. Toler was presented with a handsome hand-painted plate, and a formal luncheon, at which she "looked charming in a cream voile and chiffon satin blouse, which enhanced her brunette type of beauty."

While in town, Sidney took charge of The Acme Comedy Company, which was booked at the Toler Auditorium that summer. He reorganized the company, added some local talent, and presented his own plays – much to the delight of Wichitans, who followed his career and always enjoyed watching their talented young actor perform on stage in his hometown. Reporting on his activities, the Wichita *Eagle* said: "Mr. Toler is an old Wichita boy who has made quite a reputation as a finished actor. He is very popular on the stage in the east, where his work is better known. Mr. Toler is also a writer of short stories and has a number of plays that have been used on good royalties."

The first play that Acme presented was *Captain Tom*, a naval melodrama written by Toler. He played the title role; his wife, Vivian, played the part of Mabel Martin; and his nephew, Hooper Toler, played Juba, the Cuban boy. The play was billed as "a story of the adventures of a captain in the United States Navy during the late unpleasantness with Spain, and is laid in Cuba…. Mr. Toler will present this bill as elaborate as possible, and special scenery is now under construction and costumes have been ordered from Chicago." General admission to the performance was ten cents; reserved seats were 20 cents.

Another Toler production, *How Baxter Butted In,* drew a large and enthusiastic audience. In this four-act comedy, Sidney played the role of Baxter, "a fresh traveling man ... the way he butts in and gets busy with everything and everybody is refreshing. Every member of the company is well cast in this bill, and each one does his part in presenting a finished play."

After the last production, the Acme Company and the Toler Auditorium closed for the season. Soon afterwards, the facility was leased to J. A. Wolfe of the Wolfe Stock Company, and from then on it was called the "New Auditorium."

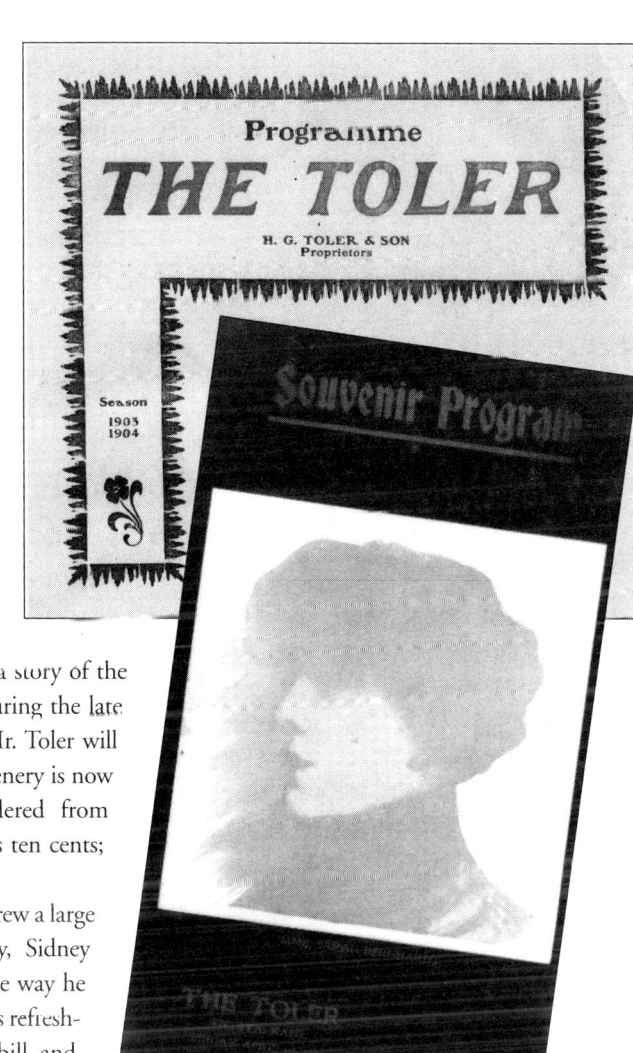

Souvenir program from actress Sarah Bernhardt's performance at the Toler Auditorium on April 6, 1906 (Tihen Collection).

In mid-July, Mr. and Mrs. Toler left Wichita for Portland, Maine, where Sidney was engaged for the month of August at a beautiful theater near the ocean. A number of his plays were hits with Eastern audiences, and favorites to be performed in Portland included *Dancing Master, Duke of Piccadilly, Belle of Richmond,* and *Captain Tom.*

Photo of Sidney Toler as Charlie Chan, c. 1935.

Note: Unattributed quotations in this article were drawn from write-ups in the Wichita *Eagle* on the occasion of Toler's visit in 1907.

"Mermaid" Made Waves in Riverside Park

Picnickers, poetry, lily ponds, and police court: Each is an element of the story behind the Wichita postcard, *The Lily Pond Mermaid*, produced in 1908 by Wichita photographer Jesse J. Todd.

It all started when a young lady named Mona, who wanted to be an artist's model like her aunt in Chicago, came to Todd's studio on North Main Street looking for such a position. Todd agreed to work with the girl and had been photographing her for about three months when he saw an Eastman Kodak advertisement offering a $1,000 prize for the best photograph of a mermaid. Todd discussed the idea with his young model, and their agreement was that she would pose for him at the Lily Pond[1] in North Riverside Park, and he would divide the prize money with her if his photo won the contest.

After securing permission from the park policeman to take photographs in the Lily Pond, Todd arrived on a Sunday morning with his camera, his model, a raincoat, and a large robe for the young lady to "spread over her while she was making the change" from her street clothes to the raincoat.

During the photo session, an early picnic party of five prominent ladies chanced to pass the Lily Pond and stopped "for about 30 to 45 minutes" to watch the proceedings. Finally, Todd later testified, he had to ask them to leave because they were bothering the model and interfering with his work. The women left, muttering something that Todd could not understand.

In court the following day, however, the ladies spoke quite distinctly, stating that the model was wearing only "the garments that nature had given her, and was posing in this condition in various positions while Todd manipulated the camera." A rude painting depicting a woman with the tail of a fish was produced to show the court how the model appeared, in at least one pose, while supposedly representing one of the mythical creatures.

Mr. George Dixon, father of one of the offended picnickers, testified that he had gone to the Lily Pond and, after finding "the girl dressed only in a raincoat, which only partially protected her body," had "requested that Todd and the young girl desist from their proceedings." To Mr. Dixon's remonstrances, Todd had responded that he was "taking better pictures than appeared in some of the bookstores of this city" and that, in addition, "he had secured the permission of the park policeman to take the pictures."

The park policeman admitted that he gave Todd permission to take photographs, as it was not an unusual request, and "many people took pictures of the place everyday." What Todd had failed to tell him was that he was going to take nude photos.

Judge Alexander stated that the photos shown in court were not considered unsuitable pictures, but that "there was an ordinance which forbade any such performance as must have taken place in the park in the securing of such postures." As a result Todd was assessed a fine of $25.

Postcard view of The Lily Pond Mermaid, c. 1908 (Tihen Collection).

Little did he know that when he decided to make a postcard from one of his negatives, his fame as an artist would increase. The Wichita *Beacon* stated: "Collectors of artistic photographs everywhere sent rush orders for mermaid pictures. Big Todds, little Todds, papa Todds and mamma Todds, have been asked to forward pictures 'at once' to anxious artists."

In fact, many people with the last name of Todd started getting photo requests because the interested parties did not know photographer Todd's first name. Such was the case with a lady in British Columbia, who collected mermaid pictures. She addressed her request to an E. Robert Todd, who was so embarrassed by the assumption that he threatened not to pass along her order.

No one knows if Todd ever won the contest or split the prize with his "mermaid." But, the postcard that resulted from the sensational photo shoot has survived – along with the following poem by the model, which appears on the back of some copies:

The Mermaid's Soliloquy

They say I am a naughty girl —
The worst in Wichita;
For the way I had my picture made,
It was against the law.

Now that good book don't say,
In Matthew, Mark, Luke or John,
That when you have a picture made,
You should have your clothes all on.

But mermaids, nymphs and fishes —
The myths of old declare,
Have no rules of etiquette,
So they have their pictures bare.

– MONA

---

[1] adjacent to the present-day Park Villa

Note: Unattributed quotations in this article were taken from the Wichita *Eagle* and the Wichita *Beacon's* reporting of this 1908 event.

"All roads lead to Wichita. All aboard." That was the slogan used by practically every railroad agent in this section of the state, and by many in Oklahoma, reported the Wichita *Eagle* in December of 1908. The Missouri Pacific, Santa Fe, Rock Island, and Frisco were all equipped with extra coaches to accommodate the crowds traveling to Wichita to do their Christmas shopping. On one day alone, the Missouri Pacific brought more than 700 people to the city on three trains. And, the evening trains leaving Wichita were filled to capacity with people loaded down with Christmas purchases.

Throughout its history, Wichita has experienced both prosperous years and lean years. The first major boom occurred in the 1880s, when homes and businesses sprang up overnight. The city grew too fast too soon, giving rise to the bust of the 1890s. By 1908, however, Wichita had recovered and was once more enjoying a period of seemingly unprecedented good fortune.

Christmas of 1908 a Wichita Merchant's Dream

The local newspapers were filled with advertisements indicating a prosperous year. The Varney Jewelry Company advertised: "'The Sign of the Time' has meant good times to us! We wish a Merry Christmas to all our friends. For a most prosperous year, we return our thanks."

Edward Vail, Jewelers and Silversmiths since 1884, displayed a marvelous array of jewelry, solid gold, and silverwares along with the following declaration: "The Great Prosperity Christmas; Never has Kansas had such marvelous crops; Never has the spirit of good will been so manifest as in this bounteous year of 1908."

Even realtors took advantage of the good times to appeal to potential buyers: "Possibly you have never given it thought, but several wives in Wichita will receive lots as Christmas presents. Wise husbands, looking into the future, realize that the time is ripe for buying sites for homes." The time to buy was now, they urged, before the city's rapid growth put a prohibitive price on property.

Furniture dealers saw a big demand in useful Christmas presents for the home: dining room suites, parlor chairs, music cabinets, davenports, bookcases, and the huge leather easy chairs that were especially popular that year – "the comfortable ones, in which hubby may retire with his new smoking jacket, the gift of the boys at the office."

An advertisement in the Sunday paper for Rorabaugh Dry Goods Company announced that they would sell 252 red steel wagons for 79 cents beginning at 8:30 Monday morning. "When the gong sounded, the procession began to move out and in exactly twenty-seven minutes the entire lot of wagons was sold. The majority of buyers were grown-ups, and they had a merry time trundling those brilliantly painted wagons through the streets."

According to Tanner's Book Store (122 North Main), the best toy of the year in 1908 was the Buckeye postcard projector. It displayed postcards, newspaper pictures, and photographs in color and was equipped for both gas and electric lights. The gas models sold for $5.00, the electric ones were $7.50, and demonstrations of both could be seen in the store.

On December 25, 1908, retail merchants "closed the most successful holiday trade season ever known in the city." Stores had been open nightly until 10:00 to accommodate customers, and many merchants interviewed by the *Eagle* reported record sales:

The Innes Department Store as it appeared in a 1911 issue of Kansas Magazine.

"Our holiday business has been much better than a year ago, and far beyond our expectations. We are entirely satisfied" (George T. Nolley Furniture Company).

"We have had all the business we could possibly handle, and it has crowded us to keep up with the orders. Our trade was much better than last year" (grocery firm of M. D. Tapp).

"The Christmas shopping season opened a week or ten days earlier with us this year. We scarcely had time to secure our goods and display them" (Walter Innes, George Innes Dry Goods Company).

"It has been our best year. There has been a noticeable increase in the state of better grade goods" (Noyes Dry Goods Company).

"During our entire twenty-two years of business in Wichita, we have never had such a Christmas season as this one. In some lines our business has increased 50 percent" (Henry Wallenstein, Boston Store).

"Our Christmas season trade this year has been better than ever before. The trade in all classes of clothing has been good, but a noticeable increase has been made in the sales of high grade clothing" (Sam Greenfield, Greenfield Brothers Clothing Store).

"We could not have taken care of any more customers if they had come. The store has been crowded most of the time, and we are all completely worn out taking care of the trade. The engraving department became so swamped with work that we were compelled to close the department two days ago. Since then we have been forced to tell customers to bring in their goods after Christmas to have engraving done" (I. F. Varney, Varney Jewelry Company).

As a contrast between the boom of the 1880s and the year 1908, a poem published in the Wichita *Sunday Growler* on December 25, 1887, is fitting to reprint here:

A Christmas Chime

Ring, ring the bells.
   Ring out a joyous chime!
Hark how the gladsome music tells –
   "This is the Christmas time!"
Gather the children in,
   Gather the poor and old;
Never one must go wandering
   On Christmas day in the cold.
'Tis Christmas in the mansion,
   The feast is grandly spread;
A sweet and toothsome morsel
   Seems this man's daily bread.
The lofty rooms are brilliant,
   The people thronging there
Are dressed in costly fabrics,
   Are gifted, young and fair.
There's ready jest and laughter,
   The viols, throbbing sweet.
Make music wild and witching
   For fairy, tripping feet.
But, oh! in all that party
   That revel there till morn,
Does ever one breathe softly,
   "Today our Lord was born."

Note: Unattributed quotations in this article were drawn from issues of the Wichita *Eagle* published during the Christmas 1908 holiday season.

Lincoln's 100th Birthday an Occasion to Reminisce

President Abraham Lincoln was a man who had personally touched the lives of many early Wichitans. Thus, in 1909, the centennial of Lincoln's birth, it was only fitting that they pause to pay tribute to him.

In honor of the occasion, catchy advertisements by local businesses contrasted the early days of Lincoln to "modern day" 1909:

"When Lincoln was a boy, practically all the studying he ever did was by the light of the old fire place." But, "... we live in the Electric Age. The latest improved electric lamp is now within the reach of practically everyone...", thanks to the Edison Light and Power Company.

"In the days of Lincoln, 'corn pone' was one of the principal articles of food. There was no such delicious and palatable food as Wolf's Honey Bread" from Wolf's Bakery in Wichita.

"Your children are more fortunate," to be able to purchase a bicycle from Central Cycle and Supply Company. "Lincoln never saw a bicycle."

And so ran the ads. Customers who patronized these businesses on the 12th of February received a free photogravure of Lincoln.

For the Wichitans who had known him, the centennial of President Lincoln's birth brought back many memories. Mrs. Monnie Moore Latham recalled her father's chair, in which Lincoln used to sit while they were neighbors in Kentucky. Her father and Lincoln had "studied by the same log fire when they were boys together." Mrs. Latham placed a high value on the chair, which she still had, and said that even though her father was a Democrat, he never allowed his political life to weaken his faith in his boyhood friend.

George Litzenberg, known as "Farmer Doolittle," met Lincoln in 1858, after "Old Abe" was nominated for United States Senator at the State Republican Convention in Springfield, Illinois. Lincoln delivered his first speech against Stephen A. Douglas at the Randolph House in Macomb, Illinois, about eight miles from where Litzenberg lived. According to Litzenberg, Douglas was "considered to have no equal on the stump, and when Mr. Lincoln met him in debate and proved his ability to take care of himself, the Republicans of the state simply went wild with delight and sung songs of 'Old Abe — Honest Abe of the West'."

Recalling what Lincoln looked like, Litzenberg said:

> …there was something attractive and pleasant in that face, and when he talked, all intelligent people knew they were in the presence of a mental giant. … I never saw that expression of sadness that people these days write so much about. From Lincoln's eyes and from his benevolent face, there always seemed to be a smile. …There was something about Mr. Lincoln which cannot be described that attracted people to him and made them call him 'Abe'. When people looked Abraham Lincoln in the face, they felt that he was good and great. He was loved and admired by his party and respected by his political opponents. He was a true patriot.

Mrs. Sarah C. Morris recalled her childhood spent in Springfield, Illinois, where her father was a wholesale tailor. "I used to take my father's checks to a place called Bunns, as I remember it, to get the money. Abraham Lincoln was nearly always there, and he used to pat me on the head and call me his little girl. He was so homely, but he just naturally had such a good look."

In sharing her memories of the president, Mrs. Sarah Honberger said: "... to have cooked dinner for Abraham Lincoln, I consider the proudest distinction of my life." In 1859, when she was 21, Sarah was living with the John English family in Reading, Pennsylvania. Being close friends, English had invited Lincoln to stay in their home while the latter was in town to give a speech. Mrs. Honberger described the visit as though it were yesterday: "Lincoln came in the morning, had dinner at noon and then went to town, where he spoke in the evening. After the speech, Mr. English and he returned and sat up until it was quite late talking over the issues of the campaign. In the morning, Lincoln arose early, ate a hearty breakfast, and left."

She also recalled that Lincoln had promised, if he was elected president, to appoint Mr. English minister to Germany:

> I was in the kitchen when he arrived. After meeting Mrs. English, he came out where I was working, shook hands with me, and asked if I wanted to go to Germany with Mr. English in case he would be appointed minister. I told him I would. ...Then he told me to be a good girl. ... There must have been something extraordinary about him, when you consider that at that time I did not realize who the big, thoughtful stranger was. ... One thing I do like to recall; he kept his word with Mr. English. After he was elected president, he appointed Mr. English to the office in Germany as he said he would. My mother would not allow me to go along, for which fact I am very sorry, as it would have been the means of my getting a better education than otherwise I was able to obtain.

A. M. Osborne added that "Lincoln was a man of deep feeling," held in esteem by the entire community for his home-like friendliness to everyone. Describing how he got to know Lincoln, Osborne said: "We settled near Salem in 1835 when Lincoln was pursuing the study of law. I went fishing and swimming at the same old mill, seventy years ago, where Lincoln went. ... When [he] was young and a surveyor, he surveyed my farm for me. I spent so many years in the vicinity of Lincoln's birthplace and know so well the early life of Lincoln that this day takes me back to my old Illinois home in the days of thirty-five."

Memories of Abraham Lincoln were vivid in the minds of many more early-day settlers. Although some of them were not Republicans, George M. Willis summed up their feelings by saying: "He was a great man, anyway, and we thought a lot of him."

Note: Unattributed quotations and advertisements in this article appeared in the Wichita *Eagle* and the Wichita *Beacon* at the time of Lincoln's Centennial celebration.

B ack in 1909, a headline in the Wichita *Eagle* declared:

JUNE – THE MONTH OF WEDDINGS
Married in the month of roses –June,
Life will be one long honeymoon.

Yesterday, like today, getting married in June was so popular as to be synonymous with tradition. As the papers all reported, that one month produced more showers for the bride-elect and more elaborate and pretty weddings than were on record for any other month.

In that day, the city's beautiful old homes were the sites of many large society weddings, like the one that took place at 8:00 p.m. on Wednesday, June 16, 1909. A prominent Wichita family, a palatial Riverside residence[1], and a lovely ceremony and reception defined

"Kirby Castle" the Setting for Classic June Wedding

the scene when Ona L. Cox, daughter of June and Tipton Cox, became the bride of Roy Hennings, son of Kathryn and Peter Hennings.

Ona Cox was an assistant piano instructor at the Wichita College of Music and prominent in music circles, having studied in New York City and at the Kelso School of Music in Chicago. The groom, at the time, was a traveling salesman for the Jett and Wood Wholesale Grocery Company, but later became secretary of the Cox-Blodgett Dry Goods Company, of which Tipton Cox was president.

Prior to the wedding, the bride was tendered showers by her close friends. At a "miscellaneous" shower, she found a gift of remembrance from each of her friends tucked in a flower bed of daisies, along with a collection of recipes entitled, "Love in a Cottage Built for Two." A two-course luncheon was served. At her kitchen- and aluminum shower, the most unusual gift Ona received was a "kitchen bride" doll: A potato masher served as the doll's body and feet, the back of a spoon formed her face, and two forks served as arms; a string dish mop substituting as hair was covered with a veil net, and a towel served as the bridal gown. Refreshments included white bride's baskets made of vanilla ice cream and filled with strawberries, light and dark cakes, and coffee.

On the eve of the wedding, the bride's parents treated the bridal party to a five-course dinner served in their home. It had only been a year since Mr. and Mrs. Cox had purchased the J. O. Davidson house — a 17-room mansion made of stone imported from Colorado and New England, which, together with the adjacent barn, occupied one city block. At the time they bought it in 1908, the house was described in the Wichita *Beacon* as "the costliest and handsomest residence property in the state of Kansas."

The house was elaborately decorated for the wedding with marguerites and greenery throughout, garlands of Dakota leaves twined in the staircase banisters, and hanging ferns and palms in the reception room. The mammoth marble fireplace in the main parlor was adorned with hanging baskets, forming an impressive backdrop for the bridal court.

At the appointed time, Mrs. Theodore Lindberg[2] sang the "Wedding March" from *Lohengrin* and descended the stairs. Behind her were the members of a vocal quartet, and following them, the wedding party. The bridesmaids were dressed in pink messaline gowns, slippers, and gloves. The maid of honor, Ona's sister Pearl, wore a gown of white satin, and the flower girl, Pauline Ayers, wore a dress of white chiffon over pink satin. The bride looked radiant in her white satin gown

The Riverside mansion built by J. O. Davidson, shown here upon its completion in 1888, became the Tipton Cox residence in 1908. In modern times, it was known as "Kirby Castle," named for longtime occupants Dr. and Mrs. G. W. Kirby, who purchased the house in 1932.

featuring a long train trimmed with duchess lace and pearl ornaments and accented by a shower bouquet of bride's roses and lilies of the valley. The groom and his best man, Ona's brother Clinton, along with the Reverend Dr. W. H. Heppe, minister of the First Methodist Episcopal Church, met the bride and her attendants at the altar.

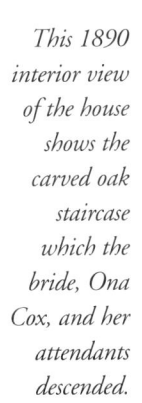

This 1890 interior view of the house shows the carved oak staircase which the bride, Ona Cox, and her attendants descended.

After the ceremony, the bridal party stood in line while congratulations were received by Mr. and Mrs. Hennings. The reception line was followed by a buffet lunch in the dining room, where the bride's colors of pink and white prevailed. Guests were entertained by the vocal quartet, the Wichita College of Music orchestra, and violin soloist Theodore Lindberg. Favors to guests were marguerites.

Wedding gifts included cut glass and silver pieces. The groom's gift to the bride was a 32nd-degree Masonic ring, set with a single diamond. To his attendants he gave laxamar cuff links. The bride gave her maid of honor a sorority ring set with diamonds and her bridesmaids each a necklace set with amethyst gems.

The bride's going-away outfit was a two-piece suit of elephant gray. The dress featured net sleeves and yoke, and the coat was accented in old rose. She wore a hat trimmed with appliqué and a red rose.

Following a three-week honeymoon trip to Colorado via the Santa Fe, the newlyweds set up housekeeping in their new two-story residence at 842 Nims.

---

[1] the J. O. Davidson Mansion at the corner of River Boulevard and Buffum, later known as "Kirby Castle" (no longer standing)
[2] an instructor at the Wichita College of Music, of which her husband was president

1911 Jubilee Included Dramatic River Show

A river festival like the one now celebrated each year in May is not new to Wichita, though it may have had a different name in the past and quite a different character. The six-day Wichita Street Fair and Carnival held in October of 1899 marked the beginning of a fall festival tradition that continued for many years. In 1908, the event was renamed the "Peerless Prophets Jubilee," and by 1911, a river pageant was part of the featured entertainment.

That year, the fourth annual Peerless Prophets Jubilee combined with the first annual Merchants Exposition to produce a mid-October spectacle billed as "the Greatest Exhibition of its kind ever held in the Southwest...." The Exposition was held in the brand new Wichita Forum[1], and (to uphold the hyperbole) the Jubilee included a carnival, an after-dark electrical float parade, band concerts, two football games (Friends University vs. Kansas State Normal School, and Fairmount College[2] vs. Washburn of Topeka), an action-packed reenactment of a famous Civil War naval battle, and a spectacular fireworks display.

Every day, crowds thronged to Ackerman's Island[3], where Patterson's Shows – advertised as "the best and cleanest carnival show on the road" – added its 20 exciting attractions to the amusements offered by Wonderland Park[4].

A highlight of one evening was the electrical float parade along Main Street and Douglas Avenue, which the newspapers described as "one of the most beautiful and elaborate ever staged in the United States." The floats were "electrically lighted" using the overhead trolley wires. All ten were drawn by elaborately draped horses, accompanied by escorts in uniforms representing the lodges of the city, and "peopled by the most beautiful women and girls of the Peerless Princess."

As the floats passed by, the throngs witnessed the passage of time from "Ancient Greece" to the "Glory of Rome" to "King Arthur's Court." Other float themes included the Pilgrims arriving at Plymouth Rock and the Indian meeting the white man; the United States depicting liberty, justice, and equality; Kansas depicting the spirit of our commonwealth; and the modern 1911 skyline of Wichita depicting the "Peerless Princess of the Plains."

A young lady named Mabel Buell rode atop the revolving "Monument to Wichita" float. Below her on four wings, each representing a stage of Wichita's spectacular growth, were an Indian, a cowboy, a mechanic, and a merchant. Coincidentally, Mabel's father was the designer of all ten floats in the parade. Both she and her brother, Horace, assisted him with the painting, and her mother did all the remaining detail work as well as the costuming.

The only thing that marred the effect was the failure to secure perfect electrical connections with the street railway trolleys. Before the parade was completed, all of the trolley poles had been broken from their fastenings.

Over at the Wichita Forum, the entertainment included Sorrentino and the Banda Rossa, "one of the largest and greatest bands touring America," which performed twice daily at 2:30 and 7:45 p.m. The crowd's favorite songs included *My Rosary*, *Rigolette*, and one of Sorrentino's own compositions entitled *Willow Grove*.

For those not interested in music, the Forum offered a number of other attractions: an industrial display, a poultry show, an agricultural exhibit, an electrical display, and numerous lectures. Also housed in the vastness of the Forum was the United States Navy exhibit, which included models of a submarine, the gunboat *Denver*, and the first-class battleship of the Atlantic squadron, *Connecticut* (the admiral's flagship of the Atlantic fleet).

The visitor with a scientific mind could also view wireless telegraphy demonstrations, which touted the invention's "novelty" and the "twentieth century miracles enacted by the use of this machine, which talks intelligibly…over ocean spaces as broad as from Wichita to New York."

This montage from the 1911 Peerless Prophets Jubilee and Merchants Exposition appeared in "Wichita: City of Opportunities," a promotional booklet published in 1912 by the Wichita Business Association (Tihen Collection).

The most dramatic event of the Jubilee, however, focused attention on a technological miracle from a previous age: the Civil War ironclad. The two most famous of these armored naval vessels, the *Merrimac*[5] and the *Monitor*, met at the mouth of the James River in Virginia on March 9, 1862. The battle that ensued was reenacted for Jubilee crowds on two consecutive nights. The action took place north of the Murdock Avenue Bridge at the bend of the Little Arkansas River, where the battle site of Hampton Roads was reproduced in miniature, complete with fortifications along the river banks. On each side of the river, grandstands to hold a thousand spectators were erected, and tickets to the production were sold for 25 cents each.

At showtime, the stands were filled to capacity, and thousands more lined the bridges, covered waterfront lawns on the east, and even climbed the trees to gain a vantage point. Attendance was not limited to Wichitans. The numbers were swelled by the "special trains and extra service on the incoming trains on all roads," which brought great crowds of out-of-towners to Wichita to witness the renowned clash between the *Merrimac* and *Monitor*. The spectacle resembled "such scenes as accompany the end of a world's series of baseball or the annual contests between the Harvard and Yale football elevens."

From the start of action at 7:15 p.m., the audience watched intently for an hour and 20 minutes as the three-act drama unfolded. Since the original battle was fought over a two-day period, the Arkansas River production featured two intermissions to denote the lapse of time.

As the first scene opened, the Confederate's *Merrimac* engaged and sank the *Congress* and the *Cumberland*. (On one of the nights, "the stern of the Cumberland refused to sink at the proper time and one of the brave soldiers was obliged to jump on it and kick it with considerable vigor before it would consent to sink according to program.")

In the second scene, the Union's *Monitor* arrived and engaged the *Merrimac* in a fierce battle. And the final act was a "celebration of the victory, with the heaviest and most beautiful fireworks ever exploded in the city."

Of all the spectators, none was more interested than Wichitan James P. Spalding. Forty-nine years earlier, in 1862, at the age of 17, he had helped build the original *Merrimac,* and afterward was the ship's carpenter. As a youth, Spalding "had stood amid a crowd of soldiers and civilians at Hampton Roads," watching the actual battle. "He heard a din of bombardment and watched the shells tearing at the frame of the Merrimac. He watched the battle with a feeling that part of his own life was being shattered in that storm of fire and smoke."

So, what did Spalding think of Wichita's 1911 reenactment on the Little Arkansas River? "The show last night on the river was a good enough miniature," he said excitedly,

> and gave the children a pretty fair idea of the real thing. But, say, now don't you tell – but that raft out there looked to me like a flat boat on the Ohio river. Now the Merrimac, the one I helped build, didn't have any railroad iron in it like these fellows say it did, but all of its iron was especially made for its use. It had a square deck with two houses on one end, and a stern chaser with a 13-inch swivel gun to pour out a stream of steel shot. And I'll tell you, and I know, the Monitor did not cause the Merrimac to retreat, as is the fixed belief nowadays.

Thinking back to March 9, 1862, when he was standing on the banks of the James River watching the battle, Spalding explained: "Old Merrimac was grounded that day and couldn't move until a couple of tugs were sent out after her, after the Monitor had moved on up the river. Her old plough was…torn off, her seams ripped open and she was grounded. The Monitor hung around and fired at her until the turret got stuck and they had to move up the river to get it fixed."

Afterward, everyone agreed that the memorable "battle of the ironclads" was a highpoint of the Jubilee. The drama was captured on film by William Barie, Jr., manager of the Marple Theater, who had recently purchased a moving picture machine and was the official photographer for the week-long celebration. His movies of the river show and other events, street scenes, and festival crowds were first shown to the public at the Marple Theater and then taken on to neighboring towns.

---

[1] precursor to Century II
[2] today, Wichita State University
[3] then located in the Arkansas River between Douglas and Second Street
[4] Wichita's first amusement park, built on Ackerman's Island. It featured a rollercoaster which was advertised as the longest in the United States at the time it was constructed in 1905.
[5] or *Merrimack*

Note: Unattributed quotations in this article appeared in issues of the Wichita *Eagle* and the Wichita *Beacon* during September and October of 1911.

"Kansas Post Card Day" a Successful Campaign in 1912

In the 19th century, advertisements enticing people to "Go West" were commonplace. But, that was not necessarily the case in the early 20th century. So, when the state's population began to wane, something was needed to motivate people to come to Kansas.

To meet this challenge, in 1912, the Kansas Development Association, under the direction of its president, Ralph Faxton of Garden City, boosted the idea of a "Kansas Post Card Day," to be observed on Kansas Day, January 29. The plan called for all citizens of Kansas to send a postcard to each of their out-of-state friends, inviting them to locate here. In this way, the entire state could join together in advertising the opportunities and resources available in Kansas. The association asked the Legislature to appropriate $50,000 to assist the effort.

Wichita became very much involved in this promotion. For one thing, the postcard was designed and painted by a Wichita artist, Coy Avon Seward. Seward, who studied art under Birger Sandzén at Lindsborg, Kansas, was manager of the Capper Engraving Company (5th floor, Butts Building, 145-149 North Lawrence[1]). Many Wichitans are familiar with his famous painting[2] of early Wichita depicting the Munger House and the Durfee Trading Post, which he created from descriptions supplied by five early pioneers.

The postcard was also manufactured by a Wichita firm. H. R. Schmidt & Co. (418 Butts Building) printed and distributed 1,000,000 copies of the Kansas card. Schmidt had started his wholesale postcard business in Wichita less than a year before, and it was growing so fast that he employed 13-15 postcard salesmen who traveled out of the city. The company advertised itself as "the largest postal card dealers west of the Mississippi." Schmidt also operated the Post Card Shop in the Schweiter Building (northeast corner of Main and Douglas), which was managed by Mr. and Mrs. Frank W. Jenkins. The Kansas postcard bore the following message:

KANSAS CALLING YOU!
EVERY INDUSTRIAL OPPORTUNITY
EVERY AGRICULTURAL OPPORTUNITY
EVERY SOCIAL AND EDUCATIONAL OPPORTUNITY
ROOM FOR A MILLION!

In addition to using the postcard for the official statewide promotion, several cities — including Topeka, McPherson, Salina, and Wichita — used Seward's card design but replaced the Kansas message with one of their own. Wichita's postcard read as follows:

WICHITA–CITY OF OPPORTUNITIES
THE CITY WITH THE BRIGHTEST FUTURE
IN THE SOUTHWEST WANTS YOU TO
SHARE HER GREAT PROSPERITY

Advertisements in the local papers urged people to boost Wichita by sending a Wichita postcard along with their Kansas postcard on Kansas Day, January 29, to commemorate the first Kansas Post Card Day. The picture of the Wichita postcard appeared in the local papers for several days.

Both the card with the state text and the card with the Wichita text were on sale for a penny apiece at the following Wichita stores: Higginson Drug Co.; Geo. Innes & Co.; F. G. Orr's Book Store; C. A. Tanner & Co.; Goldsmith's Book Store; S. H. Kress & Co.; C. A. Kessler & Co.; the Boston Store; Rorabaugh Dry Goods Co.; the Post Card Shop; and Meyers Post Card Studio. Some individuals purchased as many as 100 cards at a time.

In addition to Kansas Day, January 29 marked the observance of another, less-publicized event: McKinley Day, in honor of the birthday of martyred U.S. President William McKinley. Since the carnation was McKinley's favorite flower, Wichitans were urged to wear a carnation on January 29 in addition to sending their postcards.

Some florists included both the postcard and a picture of President McKinley in their window displays. One of the most attractive arrangements was that in the window of C. P. Mueller (145 North Main): "A large picture of the martyred president is draped in American flags, with a bowl of red carnations at one side. The Kansas Day card, enlarged, is framed in bark with an immense bunch of sunflowers placed at the top."

In spite of their efforts, McKinley Day carnation sales were apparently not in the numbers that florists had envisioned. A local newspaper reported: "People have been kept so busy sending out Kansas Day cards that they have neglected to go to the florist for their carnation in honor of the birthday of William McKinley." Perhaps, if they were upset with their carnation sales, the florists should have also sold the postcards in their shops, in order to provide more incentive to the customer.

At any rate, the first Kansas Post Card Day was a huge success, with 30,000 cards sold in Wichita alone. The postal service was kept busy sending and delivering all the cards, which could each be mailed for the price of a one-cent stamp. In subsequent years, a Kansas Post Card Day was tried again, but none of the later celebrations met with the success that the original event enjoyed.

Wichita's adaptation of the Kansas state postcard designed in 1912 for "Kansas Post Card Day" (Tihen Collection).

---

[1] now Broadway
[2] today on display at the Wichita-Sedgwick County Historical Museum (Wichita's old City Building)

Note: Unattributed quotations in this article were drawn from issues of the Wichita *Eagle* and the Wichita *Beacon* during the Kansas Post Card Day campaign of 1912.

Riverside's Park Villa: a Labor of Love

The visitor to North Riverside Park may have noticed the shelter house just southwest of the corner of 10th and Bitting – near the spot where *The Boy With the Boot* statue stood for many years – but may not be aware of its historical significance to Wichita. The shelter was built because of one woman's love and determination and a community that helped provide for its financial support.

Park Villa, or "Rest Room," as the facility was called, was the concept of Laura Buckwalter, the wife of Wichita dentist Oliver Buckwalter. Mrs. Buckwalter was a civic-minded woman, always interested in bettering life for the citizens of Wichita. When she ran for the City Commission in 1911, she received only 874 votes in the primary election; but winning that amount was a significant achievement for a woman in those days. She was a candidate for City Commissioner at least two more times, but was never elected.

Mrs. Buckwalter's special desire was to create in Riverside Park a rest area where families could cool off on hot summer days near the trees and river. She went before the City Commission many times to request funding for building the shelter, but no funds were forthcoming.

Unable to get anywhere with the city, but determined to succeed, Mrs. Buckwalter generated public support for her project and raised the necessary funds on her own. In order to keep construction costs at a minimum, the City Commissioners agreed to let the local jail prisoners build the shelter under her supervision.

The building's modified mission style and Spanish red tile roof were characteristic of the work of Ulysses Grant Charles, architect for the project. Other attractive features were the cobblestone walls, built of stones gathered from the street car tracks, and the wide porch running all around the building, which provided a generous outdoor seating area shaded from the sun. The interior space was divided among a reception hall, a kitchen and dining room for the use of picnic parties in the park, and lavatories. The cornerstone on the southeast corner of the building, laid in May of 1912, bore the following inscription:

U. G. CHARLES, Architect and Superintendent
LAURA BUCKWALTER, Contractor

On May 18, 1913, as Mrs. Buckwalter was about to see her fond hopes realized, a story entitled "What a Woman's Energy Will Do" appeared in the Wichita *Eagle*. After a suitable introduction – "Believing that recreation is the cornerstone of health, this city has liberally provided for the people the best of park and bathing systems" – the article went on to describe the new Park Villa addition: "The base of the foundation is 375 foot square. The building is re-enforced. The interior is oak finish. The name of the building is inscribed over the four entrances in black and white tile. It is located near the lily pond; the first money for it was secured in August 1911 by Mrs. Buckwalter, and the work started in May 1912."

Two weeks after the article appeared, on June 2, 1913, Park Villa was formally opened in an evening ceremony attended by more than 200 people. Rodolph Hatfield, president of the Kansas Fraternal Citizens, presided over the event. Addresses were given by City Commissioner Robert B. Campbell and Mrs. Rodolph Hatfield, representing the Federation of Women's Clubs. Special recognition was given to benefactress Laura Buckwalter and architect U. G. Charles. At the conclusion of the program, the Metropolitan Band played while the guests enjoyed refreshments.

Postcard view of Park Villa, c. 1912 (Tihen Collection).

The names of the 81 donors who made possible Park Villa's construction were inscribed in an area 8 feet x 12 feet on one of the walls of the building. Unfortunately, that panel was covered over during a remodeling project several years ago. But, H. B. Damon, a local photographer, photographed the building and listed all 81 donors on the back of the photo. They included the following firms:

    Carl Graham Wall Paper Company
    Comley Lumber Company
    Daniels Furniture Company
    Kindell Plumbing Company
    Metz Lumber Company
    Ponca Tent and Awning Company
    Riggs Hardware Company
    Steele Hardware Company
    Wichita Iron Foundry
    Wichita Sash and Door Company

Halloween of Yesteryear Was Fun for All Ages

Many years ago, Halloween was a joyous occasion – a time of merriment for young and old alike. Halloween traditions in America were based on customs of the English, Irish, and Scottish, whose celebration was described in an article that appeared in the *Sunday Growler* in 1887: "…the festivities began with a generous dinner or supper early in the evening. After dinner followed the pulling of the 'kale' of cabbage stalks, the burning of nuts, the ducking of apples, the taking of an apple with the teeth from a suspended stick, and, lastly, a grand dance."

A sampling of old Wichita newspaper articles provides a good look at how Halloween used to be celebrated here. Whatever else was going on, between the years of 1908 and 1925, dances and pumpkin pie seemed to prevail.

One of the best parties of the season in 1908 took place at the Country Club[1], a favorite spot among Wichitans for entertaining guests. In the dining room, autumn vines and palms, yellow chrysanthemums, and Halloween lanterns placed over electric lights provided holiday atmosphere for 100 guests, who enjoyed dinner and background music by Bamberger's Orchestra. Afterward, tables were set up in an upstairs room for the card party hosted by Mrs. Ralph Lockwood and Mrs. John Burns. Favors awarded for "top notch" were a dainty Doulton plate to Mrs. Carl Highbarger and a glass desk set to Mr. Butler. Guests also enjoyed dancing to Bamberger's Orchestra from 8:30 to 11:30 p.m.

The popular Bamberger orchestra returned to the Country Club to play for a Halloween dance hosted by Mrs. Harry Gee and Mrs. A. H. Dickinson at which 60 guests were present.

Another festive event was the country-themed "Rube" party given by Mr. and Mrs. Hartman at the Dancing Academy. The hall was decorated with cornstalks, fodder, and hay to create a rustic, outdoor effect. Lads and lasses came to the party dressed in overalls, sunbonnets, and aprons (even the orchestra was dressed up), and prizes were awarded for the best costumes. Later, everyone enjoyed dancing the country polkas and quadrilles.

Those not invited to the Country Club or another private party could attend the masquerade party at Wonderland Park[2]. At the skating rink, over 150 of the 300 skaters were in disguise, and prizes were awarded for the best lady's and best man's costumes.

For the younger set, a "ghost and goblin party" was hosted by Miss Pauline Walters at 140 South Hydraulic. Rooms were decorated with cut flowers and ferns, and pumpkin-headed ghosts were plentiful in the parlor and sitting room. After playing games and telling ghost stories, the children went for a trolley ride to the cemetery at Ninth and Hillside and through the Fairmount addition, encountering numerous ghosts along the way.

Mr. and Mrs. May hosted a "jolly ghost party" in the attic of their residence at Wabash and Second Street, where a fortune teller held "full sway." Guests also enjoyed games, music, and refreshments of pumpkin pie and punch.

Another children's party was sponsored by the Endeavor Society of the South Lawrence Christian Church[3]. The invitation read:

Assembly of Ghosts
at Haunted House in Spook Valley,
Friday Evening, October 30.
Train leaves 1126 South Market Street.

At 7:45 p.m., the ghosts "all garbed in white sheets" boarded the streetcar for the "Haunted House" (a vacant house in the north part of the city). When they arrived, the children were greeted "with groans and screeches" and then were escorted through the house, which was "weirdly lighted with fantastical pumpkin faces, from which came the faint light of a candle." On the upper floor, each guest was held firmly by the hands of two great ghosts and "hurried down shaking stairs to the rear of the haunted house, where another strange being in white was awaiting their arrival." After this endurance test, all masks were taken off, and everyone enjoyed the rest of the evening popping corn and playing games.

Friends University "was the scene of many weird and 'witchy' revelries." The "Prince of Darkness," with his numerous attendants, "held a high court of carnival in the great chamber of mysteries." Afterward, everyone unmasked and enjoyed a lunch of sandwiches, pumpkin pie, apples, and coffee, and the playing of games, which included bobbing for apples.

Several years later, in 1914, Mrs. Sam Woolard, 708 North Lawrence Avenue[4], hosted a meeting of the members of the Daughters of the American Revolution during the Halloween season. Miss Harriet Stanley gave a talk on Belgium illustrated with cards and slides, and Mrs. Charles Hatton performed several vocal numbers. The rooms were darkened, and lighted jack-o-lanterns cast a soft glow over everything, creating an eerie atmosphere for singing songs and enjoying pumpkin pie, doughnuts, and coffee.

For the Matinee Tea held at Halloween time in 1919, waitresses at the Innes Tea Room were dressed in yellow crepe, with yellow ribbon anklets tied around their white hose just above the ankle.

Two children's parties in 1922 were unique. Master Paul Cline and Miss Mary Cline were the little host and hostess for a Halloween wiener roast at their residence at 526 West Central Avenue. Twenty-two children enjoyed the evening, which included a gypsy fortune teller. And, Miss Naomi Ketcham and Albert Hurst entertained with an old-fashioned barn dance at the Ketcham residence at 412 North Market. The garage of the residence was decorated with cornstalks, jack-o-lanterns, ghosts, and broom sticks. Cider and doughnuts were served to 20 guests.

The year 1925 was filled with Halloween celebrations. The Kansas Gas and Electric Company hosted a Halloween dance and costume party for employees and their families. Prizes were awarded for the most artistic costume, the best domino costume, the most comical costume, the most original costume, and the best-costumed couple. Refreshments of doughnuts and cider were served.

Misses Grace and Mable Williams, who lived at 1102 North Topeka, also hosted a dance. The party rooms were decorated with black cats, witches, and jack-o-lanterns, and a lively orchestra provided music. A cat dance, a balloon dance, and unusual party favors added to the evening's entertainment.

That same year, the Wichita *Eagle* sponsored its first annual Halloween party in the downtown district. "Thousands lined the streets to witness a mammoth prize costume parade." According to the paper, this was one of the biggest parties ever held in Kansas. The parade started at 9:00 p.m. and included over "200 costumed contestants headed by a squad of motorcycle police, the Wichita Mexican Band, and the beautiful float depicting 'The Spirit of Halloween'." The three judges – one each from the Boston Store, the Geo. Innes Co., and the Dockum Drug Co. – awarded cash prizes of $15.00, $10.00, and $5.00 for the three best Halloween costumes, and $10.00, $5.00, and $3.00 for the first, second, and third most grotesque costumes. During the evening, a concert featured "the Mexican Band under the direction of Prof. Antonio dé la Mora."

These activities are but a representative sampling of the many festivities that once took place in our city at Halloween time. How wonderful it would be if Wichita could only return to the era of fun and safe Halloween parties.

---

[1] then located at English and Hammond Drive, at the east end of present-day College Hill Park
[2] on Ackerman's Island in the Arkansas River between Douglas and Second Street
[3] today, Broadway Christian Church
[4] now Broadway

Note: Unattributed quotations in this article were taken from write-ups appearing in the Wichita *Eagle* during the Halloween season of 1908.

Balloon Race Thrust Wichita into National Spotlight

On October 7, 1915, Wichita hosted a national balloon race. Races had already been held in such cities as St. Louis, Kansas City, and Portland, Oregon, and enthusiasm for the sport was riding high.

All eyes were on Wichita as aeronauts and dignitaries from aero clubs across the country convened to participate in the latest race, sponsored by the newly-organized Wichita Aero Club. Among the guests was Robert M. Thompson, who represented the Naval Aviation League of America in Washington, D.C.

Five balloons were entered in the Wichita competition: the *Dayton*, piloted by William Rasor of Brookville, Ohio; the *Kansas City*, piloted by John Watts of Kansas City; the *St. Louis*, piloted by William Assmann of the St. Louis Aero Club; the *Wichita I*, piloted by Paul MCullough of the St. Louis Aero Club; and the *Wichita II*, owned and piloted by Capt. H. E. Honeywell of the St. Louis Aero Club, "one of the most famous balloon pilots in the world."

The balloons were launched from the baseball park adjacent to Wonderland Park[1]. Starting time was set at 5:00 p.m. "in order to give the aeronauts the advantage of a full capacity of gas with which to fly the low temperature at night." It took 280,000 cubic feet of natural gas to inflate the balloons, each of which was equipped with an altimeter to register the altitude, a statoscope to indicate the rise or descent, sand ballast, and an iron anchor to aid in landing. The pilots were also provided with a supply of telegraph blanks and "heavy" envelopes so that, in case of an emergency, a brief message could be written (the weight of a few ounces of sand would cause the envelope to drop to the ground, and the finder was to take it to the nearest telegraph office).

At the start, the *Dayton* failed to inflate properly, and it never got off the ground. The *Kansas City* landed only three miles east of Derby, Kansas, and finished fourth. Pilots Rasor and Watts each received $100 to help cover their expenses.

Wichita I, the newest balloon in the race, landed 20 miles east of Winfield, Kansas, and came in third. The Wichita Aero Club had recently purchased the balloon from the French-American Balloon Company for $850 and christened it just prior to launch. Unfortunately, the gas bag caught on a wire fence during the landing and was damaged. Pilot McCullough received $200 and a trophy for his third place finish.

Second place went to the silver-colored *Wichita II*, which landed near Goshen, Arkansas. Pilot Honeywell was assisted in his flight by Delos P. Woods, president of the Wichita Aero Club. Honeywell received a second-place trophy and $300 – plus a silver trophy offered by the St. Louis Aero Club to the balloon that landed nearest St. Louis. (Upon arriving back in Wichita, Woods was heard to say, "Short flights are fun, but keep away from long-distance races.")

The yellow *St. Louis* won the race, descending in a cotton field southeast of Prescott, Arkansas. For placing first, pilot Assmann received $400 and three trophies

An entry in the Wichita Aero Club's balloon race held in 1915 in conjunction with the Wichita Wheat Show.

Aerial view of Ackerman's Island taken from a balloon during the 1915 race.

for the greatest distance (363 miles), highest altitude (13,000 feet), and longest time in the air (over 19 hours).

Reporting on the October 7 spectacle, the Wichita *Beacon* boasted: "We pulled off one of the biggest events in the history of the city and entertained 10,000 people. Hundreds of newspapers all over the United States have been printing news of the race and Wichita has received much valuable publicity."

The city's first balloon race was an event not soon forgotten by Wichitans. "It was a pretty sight with four balloons sailing southeast over the city at the same time." Kodaks and cameras clicked, and the Pathé Motion Picture Company captured the flight on film. In fact, the first aerial views of Wichita stem from this competition — some of which still exist, thanks to the family of Delos P. Woods.

---

[1] on Ackerman's Island in the Arkansas River

Note: Unattributed quotations in this article were taken from the Wichita *Eagle* and the Wichita *Beacon's* coverage of the October 7, 1915, race.

Thanks to Walter P. Innes, of the Innes Dry Goods Company, the Wichita Fire Department was one of the first fire departments in the United States to become motorized. Believing that the city rated a first-class, modernized fire department, in 1909, he and supporter Howard Wheeler circulated petitions requesting the City Commission to purchase new, up-to-date equipment. Explained Innes: "I figured that the Wichita fire department was so well thought of by the citizens of Wichita that we should do all we could to keep the department at the front in modern equipment."

In the early days, fire equipment was horse-drawn. After the turn of the century, the experienced horses were all up in years; and, in 1906, an article in the Wichita *Eagle* said they were "too slow and…not fitted for the sudden runs which they are called to make.… Some of them are very old and will soon have to be relieved from active duty."

Four years later, in 1910, the City Commission contracted with the Webb Motor Fire Engine Company of St. Louis, Missouri, to build a modern fire-fighting machine at a cost of $5,750.00. The machine, it was announced, was to be a combination chemical hose wagon and engine. "It will have a complement of 1,000 feet of fire hose, 200 feet of chemical hose, two large chemical tanks, a sixty-horsepower engine, ladders, axes and other equipment." Fire Chief A. G. Walden predicted that the Wichita Fire Department would be horseless in two years.

Drive to Motorize Fire Department Signaled End of Era

While it wasn't accomplished quite that quickly, the use of horse-drawn fire apparatus at the central station (109-113 East William) did become a thing of the past on April 18, 1914, with the arrival of the last of three new pieces of motor equipment: a 90-horsepower motorized hose wagon with coupling bar to draw the engine. By 1916, there were only seven horses still in use, and they were kept at suburban stations[1].

During the summer of 1916, a group called the Alcine Players was contracted to play at the Crawford Theater. On July 4-8, they paid tribute to the horse-drawn era with their presentation of *The Still Alarm*, one of the most popular and successful melodramas written by Joseph Arthur[2]

Produced as a benefit for the Wichita Firemen's Relief Fund, *The Still Alarm* portrayed the professional and home lives of New York firemen prior to the days of motorized equipment. It embodied all that was essential in a good melodrama, including the hero and heroine, and the elements of love, honor, and devotion. Presented in four acts, the production utilized special, elaborate scenery and included new effects not before attempted on stage.

Appearing along with the Alcine Players were some Wichita firemen, including Capt. W. R. Snow, Charles Duffner, H. E. Morehead, and Earnest Matherly, plus two veteran horses, *Tom* and *Dick*, who were the last big roan team to serve Wichita at station no. 6. Together, they introduced the audience to a real and properly-equipped fire station, an alarm, and the quick hitch-up and getaway routine.

Photo of the Wichita Fire Department's central station adjacent to the City Building on William, c. 1911

The climax of the drama depicted the firemen in their beds upstairs and *Tom* and *Dick* munching on hay in their stalls. When the "still alarm" sounded, firefighters and steeds sprang into action. The men leaped from their beds, donning raiment and sliding down the steel poles. The horses jumped to their places under the harness, and the firemen hitched the team to the fire engine. Then, amid the clanging of bells and shouting of commands, the equipment raced across the stage on its way to the fire, while the audience went wild with applause at the quick response to the alarm.

The production drew record crowds, and special matinee performances were held to accommodate them all. The Wichita Fire Department alone sold over 1,000 tickets, which ranged in price from 10 to 50 cents. Referring to the tribute, Assistant Fire Chief Al Brownewell said, "it is the last button on Gabe's coat because only a few months more and the horse-drawn apparatus will be a thing of the past in Wichita. There are lots of Wichita people and especially children who have never seen the fire horses work."

Not only for the audience, but also for the Wichita Fire Department, it must have been an emotional time. Prior to the event, the Wichita *Beacon* had reported that the run to be made in the engine house scene would be "…in the nature of a farewell performance for the big roans. This is their last year in the service. Motorized equipment will crowd them out next year. For ten years they have been the pride of the service." At the end of each production, *Tom* and *Dick* received standing ovations.

There was also a guest appearance by retired fire horse *Old Ginger*, who had been coached to execute an original stunt in two of the performances. Then 23 years old, *Old Ginger* had served the fire department for 17 years, working at every station in the city and in every harness in the department – even drawing the chief's buggy – and had never missed one fire call.

---

[1] The last one to use horses was station no. 6 on the southeast corner of South Lawrence (now Broadway) and Bayley.
[2] who also wrote *The Cherry Pickers, Lost River,* and *On the Wabash*

Note: Unattributed quotations in this article were taken from issues of the Wichita *Eagle* and the Wichita *Beacon* in 1909 and 1916.

Helen Keller Made Lasting Impression on Wichita Audience

Of all the famous people who have spoken and performed in Wichita's churches and auditoriums, Helen Keller was one of the most unforgettable. Brought here by the City Federation of Women's Clubs as part of their educational program, Miss Keller delivered her message on "Happiness" to a packed house at the Central Church of Christ[1] the night of February 2, 1916. Tickets were sold at Dockum's Drug Store for 25, 35, 50 and 75 cents. The lecture was a sell-out, and more than 300 people were turned away at the door.

At 8:00 p.m., Mrs. Anne Macy, Helen's teacher and constant companion, stepped up to the platform and introduced the audience to her world famous pupil: Miss Keller was born in 1880 in Tuscumbia, Alabama, and had been blind and deaf since the age of 19 months. By the time she was seven, she could read and write. When she was ten years old, she could speak. And, at the age of 16, she was preparing for college!

Mrs. Macy explained how Helen learned to communicate through years of ceaseless effort and determination: "Miss Keller 'hears' through the touch of her hand. By placing the thumb on the larnyx, the first finger on the lips, and the second finger on the nose, she feels all the vibration of the vocal organs ... and after years of study managed to make out a vocabulary from her sense of touch."

"Today," she concluded, Miss Keller has "accomplished everything that scientists said she would never be able to do: graduated with honors from Radcliffe College, written several books, and actually delivered a lecture. This was said, by great aural surgeons, to be the greatest individual achievement in the history of education."

The lecture delivered by Helen Keller that evening was inspiring and full of sunshine, optimism, and a "Pollyanna" cheer. She told her Wichita audience:

> God has been very good to me. He has put into my heart the joys of living, and even though I can't see or hear, I know of the beauty and the goodness of the world. ... Happiness depends upon yourself. If we have the will and a faith in God, we all can be happy. Happiness and peace of mind are like the flowers. No matter how small the opportunities of happiness, it will do some good for mankind. To be really happy we must have more love, more justice, more devotion. We should live so others could feel better and happier.

Photo of the church where Helen Keller spoke, c. 1915.

When Mrs. Macy asked Helen to repeat the *23rd Psalm*, she spoke "slowly, distinctly and with an abundance of feeling." She then backed "away from the platform, felt her way to the altar and there with her hands outstretched and looking toward the heavens through eyes that see not, she made an impressing figure as she cried out."

Following her lecture, and with the help of her teacher, Helen answered questions from the audience. "I can judge people I meet by the grip of their hands," she said. "I form an opinion of them at once. Sometimes I guess their secrets, too." Such was the case with one young man Helen shook hands with. She knew he was in love; and, when she asked him, he told her he had been married four months.

Helen's message to the girls of Wichita was: "I think a blind girl can choose just as good a husband as those who can see. I know I can tell a lot by feeling the hand, and if girls felt their sweethearts' hands more than they looked at their clothing and their dressy make-up, better husbands might be in the making."

When asked if she liked music, Helen replied, "Oh, yes, I love music. I feel the different musical vibrations all over my body, and I rejoice in it. I love *Yankee Doodle*." Admitting that her favorite poet was Walt Whitman, Helen said, "His poems thrill and glow with that new brotherhood and joy of which all men dream." When questioned about what language she liked the best, she replied, "My own, and from the rest I think I prefer French; then German." And, when asked what was the most worthwhile thing in life, she responded, "Service to our fellow men."

After the program, Helen, Mrs. Macy, and her secretary, Miss Polly Thompson, were escorted out the back door and put into a taxi, which took them to the Eaton Hotel where they were guests for the night. The next morning, the three boarded the train for Coffeyville, Kansas, the next stop on Helen's lecture tour.

Her visit was a big success for the City Federation of Women's Clubs, and Wichita was grateful for the chance to have hosted a speaker the caliber of Helen Keller, who had been drawing record crowds and was one of the highest salaried lecturers in the country at that time. The $300 that Helen received for her appearance, like the money raised by all her speaking engagements, went to aid others who were blind.

---

[1] southeast corner of Second and Market

Note: Unattributed quotations in this article were drawn from the Wichita *Eagle* and the Wichita *Beacon's* coverage of Miss Keller's 1916 visit to Wichita.

Henry Lassen Hailed as a "Public Utility"

Wichita was stunned when Henry Lassen passed away on January 3, 1919, at the age of 58. His new hotel had just been dedicated on New Year's Eve, and a dinner in his honor was scheduled to take place on the 10th of January.

At the time of his death, Lassen was president of the Kansas Milling Company, the Hotel Lassen, the Wichita Terminal Grain Elevator Company, and the Mid-Continent Tire Manufacturing Company, and a director of the Guarantee Title & Trust Company, the Arkansas Valley Interurban Company, Midland Valley Railway Company, and the Board of Commerce. He was a past president of the Wichita Commercial Club, the Traffic Bureau, Southwestern Millers' League, and Southern Kansas Millers' Club, and a stockholder in numerous other enterprises. His worth at the time was estimated to exceed $1,000,000.

Henry Lassen was the embodiment of the self-made man. Born in Schleswig, Denmark, in 1861, he emigrated to America at the age of 17, arriving in this country a pauper. As stated in his obituary, "… he became within 40 years the greatest miller in the Southwest and one of the most prominent in the entire country. His counsel was sought not only by millers and grain men, but by many others who recognized him as an astute and careful business man in general."

Lassen became interested in milling and the grain business after arriving in America. He first operated a mill in Nebraska. After the land rush in 1889, he moved to Guthrie, Oklahoma. In 1903, he and Charles Moore Jackman opened the Canadian Mill and Elevator Company at El Reno, Oklahoma. They sold the business in 1905 and moved to Wichita the following spring.

Intending to build a mill, the partners purchased land at Santa Fe and 13th Street. Their plans called for a milling capacity of 1,500 barrels of flour per day and an elevator capacity of 300,000 bushels of grain. On June 15, 1906, the Wichita *Eagle* reported: "When completed, the mill and elevator will be the largest of the kind in the state." The enterprise became known as the Kansas Milling Company, of which Lassen was president and general manager and Jackman was secretary-treasurer. After Lassen died, Jackman assumed the duties of president and general manager.

For several days following his death, the local newspapers were filled with praise for Henry Lassen. On January 9, 1919, members of the Board of Commerce reported in the Wichita *Beacon*:

> Wichita has lost one of her great commercial assets. As a town builder Henry Lassen stood supreme. No greater compliment could be paid to his commercial genius, as Wichita is more than ordinarily pleased with capable, public-spirited, business men.
>
> … Henry Lassen served Wichita at a great personal sacrifice. …Warned repeatedly by his physicians to curtail his activities and to seek rest and relaxation, yet he could not resist the call to action when some enterprise for the good of Wichita lagged for the want of support. …The great institutions created by his efforts in Wichita will stand, therefore, literally as monuments to his genius as a town builder, and the commercial interests of this city will long mourn his loss; the loss of the friendship of so lovable a character, as well as his leadership in all things that aided to make Wichita a fortunate city in which to live.

Bronze memorial plaque honoring Henry Lassen, which hung in the Lassen Hotel lobby for many years.

The Kansas City *Star* reported: "Henry Lassen was a successful man. He had built up one of the biggest milling industries in the country. He was the kind of a successful man who knew how to use his resources. He was one of the most enterprising citizens of Kansas and a leader in all business enterprises in Wichita. He was an inspiration to the city and the state."

It was Henry Lassen who encouraged Henry J. Allen to run for governor. Governor-elect Allen paid him a glowing tribute, reported by the *Beacon*, when he referred to Lassen as a "public utility." Whenever a project lacked financial support, Lassen could be depended upon to support it, said Allen: "I have seen few happier men than Henry Lassen was New Year's eve when they opened the Hotel Lassen and the dream which the community had been dreaming so long came true. There was no vanity or self-gratification in the moment for him. His joy was that the community possessed the thing it had longed for and that he had been able to help bring it about, and the community accepted the gift of his services in the spirit in which those services had been given."

Although the dinner in honor of Henry Lassen was not held, his friends and associates wanted to recognize his generosity in a very special way. So, they commissioned the Gorham Company of New York, one of the leading foundries in the United States at the time, to make a bronze memorial tablet, which featured a sculpture of his face bolted to the plaque. When completed, the tablet was placed in the Lassen Hotel lobby, where it hung for many years before being donated to the Wichita-Sedgwick County Historical Museum.

Recently, the plaque was restored to its original finish by the Westwood Bronze Memorials Company of Wichita. Jay Westwood admitted he had never seen anything like the Lassen piece, but he knew it was unique and had to have been very expensive to make.

Note: Unattributed quotations in this article appeared in the Wichita *Beacon* on January 3, 1919.

Wichitans who have never noticed the memorial drinking fountain on the curb at the northeast corner of Third and Main might want to examine this historic monument the next time they are in the area.

The fountain was erected in 1922 to provide drinking water for the public and to mark the original site of the Wichita *Eagle*, established 50 years before, on April 12, 1872, by Col. Marshall M. Murdock – a name synonymous with Wichita history.

Colonel Murdock was a politician and newspaperman from Burlingame, Kansas, who was urged by town boomers to come to Wichita and start a paper. When the opportunity was right, he made the move. From the time he arrived, Murdock had a vision of a growing and prosperous city. Through his paper, he promoted Wichita as an equal to Kansas City, Chicago, or any Eastern metropolis (at building public confidence, Colonel Murdock was unsurpassed), and he played a major role in Wichita's development from a prairie town into a city.

Fountain Recalls Founding of the Wichita *Eagle*

On Monday, October 2, 1922, at 3:00 p.m., the drinking fountain was dedicated to the City of Wichita by employees of the *Eagle*. Invitations had been sent out to those pioneers who were here when the paper was first published, and seats were erected for them at the dedication. Pioneers attending included James Cairnes, William Finn, Samuel G. Gribi, Kos Harris, David Leahy, Dan Parks, Finlay Ross, Henry Schweiter, O. B. Stocker, Otto Weiss, and Mr. and Mrs. George Whitney. Many shared their favorite stories and memories with the crowd.

County Commissioner Syl Dunkin told of having to haul the printing press and type to Wichita from Newton, Kansas, because that was as far as the railroad went at the time. Judge William C. Little recalled advertising his law firm, Atwood and Little, on page one of the first issue.

City Judge W. P. Campbell, who had turned his court over to Senator O. H. Bentley in order to attend the ceremony, recalled his first Christmas in Wichita, in 1869, "when he defended a man accused of murder. The court was held in the Durfee Ranch House."

Dr. Andrew Fabrique, the sole survivor of Wichita's first city government, recalled that the newspaper office and his residence on the southwest corner of Lawrence[1] and Central were both built by Miles and Hunter. He also enjoyed relating how his little daughter (Mrs. Mattie Nolley, also present at the ceremony) "wandered away one day, and ... her mother went across the prairie to Third and Main, and found the child playing on the outside stairs of the first Eagle building."

Aware that the office lacked the first five issues of volume one of the paper, John Davidson, a pioneer lumberman, brought along his own copies to share at the ceremony.

Judge Henry C. Sluss, whose law office was located on the upper story of the original *Eagle* building – a story-and-a-half wooden business structure that faced on Third Street and stood 50 feet east of the corner – was allowed to take the first drink from the new fountain in honor of his long, close association with Colonel Murdock.

Sidney D. Long, *Eagle* business and circulation manager, spoke on behalf of the employees in presenting the fountain to Marcellus M. Murdock, son of Marshall Murdock and current publisher of the paper. Long said, "It is with great love in the heart of each employee in the arranging of this monument. It is with a deep gratitude that we all join in presenting this monument to you."

Postcard view of the Eagle memorial drinking fountain erected in 1922 (Tihen Collection).

Marcellus Murdock then presented the fountain to the city:

> It is with great swelling pride that I join with you in this solemnly reverential yet gloriously joyful communion — a communion of those here today with the spirits of those who have gone before. ... In commemorating this parcel of ground in the presence of these many living witnesses who knew it once as an undefined portion of a seemingly limitless expanse of prairie and buffalo grass, it would be trite for me of a later generation to remark concerning the many changes about this corner. ...What changes the years have wrought. When The Eagle was founded, Chicago was just reckoning up the losses of its great two hundred million dollar fire; Morse, the father of the telegraph, had died ten days before, General Grant was in the White House and Horace Greeley of the New York Tribune was being futilely groomed to succeed Grant. ... It is the hope of all of us that in the city's receiving this fountain it will accept it not only as a marker of one of the important points in Wichita's history but, let it be a starter for many more such memorials marking for the interest and edification of the citizenship those points of historical importance to the city.

Another son, Victor Murdock, who was a United States Congressman, was unable to attend the ceremony but sent greetings and congratulations in the following message: "It strikes me as a fitting libation to the prairies after fifty years of promise and performance in Kansas, the land of sun and sky, the center of the bread basket of the world, friend to all mankind and foe to man's eternal enemy, famine."

Mayor W. C. Coleman accepted the fountain on behalf of the city. Although he was not around in the early days, he had the good fortune of knowing Marsh Murdock and paid him a glowing tribute:

> We are all heirs of the work of those sturdy pioneers who were the builders of Wichita. It is well that we pause to do homage to those tireless laborers who came out of the east and settled in the west with hopeful hearts through all discouragements and vicissitudes that we are able to enjoy the blessings of today. ...Wichita is proud of its pioneers and none stands higher in the esteem of the citizens than Col. Murdock. ...We should be glad for these markers of historic spots in Wichita linking the past with the present. ... I am glad to accept this monument to Col. Marsh Murdock and The Eagle for the city of Wichita and in doing so I recall that one of the last things Col. Murdock urged upon the people of Wichita was loyalty to law and law enforcement. That was another day, but the need for that same loyalty to law and law enforcement is still present.

The fountain, originally 2-1/2 feet tall, was carved from granite rock and bears a bronze plaque. While it stands as a monument to Wichita's past, the fountain is no longer functional, the water having been turned off some years ago.

---

[1] now Broadway

Note: Unattributed quotations in this article were taken from the Wichita *Eagle's* coverage of the fountain dedication ceremony on October 2, 1922.

Silent Screen Actress Dreamed of Wichita Movie Studio

There are many fascinating women from Wichita's past who should be written about, and silent screen film actress Jesse Fenneberg is certainly one of them.

Born in Lafayette, Indiana, in 1878, Jesse moved to Wellington, Kansas, with her parents in the 1890s. She was the belle of the town during her high school years, and at age 17, she married Frank Six, a local jeweler.

Finding herself a widow just a few years later, Jesse began touring Kansas, singing in concerts. After her father died, she persuaded her mother to go with her to California, and in 1910, they boarded a train for Hollywood. While visiting the Pathé Studios, Jesse was hired for a role in the western movie, *Rodeo*.

Jesse carried on her show business career under the stage name "Pat Miller." She appeared with Bebe Daniels in *Marked Dollar* and co-starred with Charlie Chaplin in three movies, one being *Charlie and the Devil*. She also appeared with Theda Bara, Laurel and Hardy, William Desmond, and Fatty Arbuckle.

The story of how she got the part with Charlie Chaplin is one Jesse loved to tell. It seems that her apartment at the time was near a Japanese garden where she picked fresh vegetables. One rainy day, she took refuge on a porch, which she found out was Chaplin's. "He asked me if I would like to make a movie with him, and told me he would pick me up in a carriage at my place the next day. ... I almost refused because I had a date with the doctor whom I had met while he was fixing my neighbor's broken arm a few days before, but I finally decided to go." Commenting on the experience, Jesse said: "Charlie was such a perfectionist. He had to have everything done just right and was rather hard to work with."

In a 1961 interview, Jesse spoke of how the movie industry had changed: "We very seldom knew the name of the picture we were making. They rewrote as they went along, and it might turn out to be an entirely different story from the one we started, with a new name. ...The actors took their own clothing along on location. There were no wardrobes and makeup men. We powdered our own faces." She admitted during the interview that she really "didn't care about being an actress and wasn't serious about [her] career."

After commuting for ten years between Hollywood and Wichita, Jesse settled in Wichita permanently in 1920 and married Louis Fenneberg, a pharmacist and drug salesman. They opened the Sunflower Pictures Corporation and operated a cinema school in their home at 444 North St. Francis, which was the first of its kind in Kansas. Jesse wrote and directed three local movies – *Repaid*, *Solid Ivory*, and *Relative Blues* – and produced a stage show, *Movie Madness*. Some of

Colonial Theatre, c. 1917, which became one of the first movie theaters in Wichita.

her students went on to Hollywood to appear in movies.

Plans were drawn up to enlarge her corporation on a 30-acre tract north of the city, where Hollywood stars could make movies. Unfortunately, "Hollywood on the Kansas Plains" remained a dream because of a series of tragedies which followed: Her mother suffered paralysis and required much of her time; her husband fell ill and died; and Jesse suffered a heart attack and went blind for a while, during which time her house caught fire and burned.

"Finally I just gave up my dreams for a movie city at Wichita," she said, and she settled down to writing. Her books included *Keys to the Golden West*, a novel about John C. Lockwood, a survivor of the Little Big Horn Battle. At the time of her death in 1969, she was writing her autobiography.

Jesse Fenneberg was a member of the First Methodist Church, the Twentieth Century Club, Eastern Star, and the YWCA. She is buried in Wichita's historic Maple Grove Cemetery[1].

---

[1] northeast corner of Ninth and Hillside

Note: Unattributed quotations in this article appeared in the Wichita *Eagle* and *Beacon Magazine* on October 16, 1961.

A. A. Hyde Honored for Global Generosity

In every generation of its existence, Wichita has had its great benefactors. One who came early and stayed late was Albert Alexander Hyde. On his 77th birthday, a grateful city convened to honor this man, whose life was an inspiration and a blessing to the multitude.

A. A. Hyde came to Wichita in 1872 as a bank cashier. He prospered during the boom of the 1880s but went bankrupt during the bust that followed. He rebounded financially by forming a partnership and establishing the Yucca Soap Company. From there, he went on to develop Mentholatum – "The Little Nurse for Little Ills." Hyde made a fortune from the product and shared his enormous profits with the world: Schools, colleges, churches, youth camps, and the YMCA, both locally and worldwide, benefitted from Hyde's generosity. Black, white, Hispanic, and Oriental alike were objects of his Christian concern.

On March 2, 1925, the world gathered at Hyde's feet to repay him with praise. The Wichita Forum[1] was the site of his birthday celebration, which began at 6:00 p.m. with a banquet for 1,150 invited guests. The main floor of the Forum was packed with 11 tables each 100 feet long. It took 110 members of the Business and Professional Women's Club to serve the meal prepared by Wolf and Parrott's Cafeteria, which was topped off by a cake two feet high and three feet in diameter.

After the banquet, the doors were opened to the public. Approximately 3,000 people attended the 8:00 p.m. program to honor a man who had been "the only 365-day-a-year Santa Claus that Wichita has ever had, and there is no charity in our community but that has felt the support of his benevolence." Those were the words that Henry J. Allen, editor of the Wichita *Beacon* and former Kansas governor, used to characterize Hyde in his keynote address entitled "Mr. A. A. Hyde as a Citizen."

C. Q. Chandler, chairman of the First National Bank, was toastmaster to an audience that boasted 180 out-of-town guests representing 14 states, including William E. Sweet, former governor of Colorado, and Richard Morse, 84, of New York, the oldest secretary of the YMCA. Among the prominent Kansans in attendance were William Allen White and five college presidents.

A pageant entitled *To Everyman — A Visualization*, with a cast of 200, was followed by the unveiling of a bronze bust[2] of Hyde done by Walter A. Vincent of the Western Lithograph Company.

Following Allen's keynote address, Dr. John R. Mott, international secretary of the YMCA from New York, spoke about "Mr. A. A. Hyde as a World Influence." Mott said, "I could not name one of the 58 nations of the world which I have traveled over the past 20 years where I have not seen the great influence which has come forth from the life of A. A. Hyde."

Telegrams and letters of greetings to Mr. Hyde from friends worldwide were read, and souvenir books recounting Hyde's life were handed out to guests. Music for the affair was provided by the American Legion Band.

When Mr. Hyde was introduced to convey appreciation for the evening's event, he stated: "I personally am not worthy of this attention you give me, but I appreciate the fact that the principles underlying my interest in Christianity do merit attention, and so it is these principles you are recognizing rather than the man who stands for them."

Photo of Albert Alexander Hyde, c. 1930

A. A. Hyde died on January 10, 1935, at age 86, and was buried in Maple Grove Cemetery[3], which he helped to lay out. Today, Wichitans are reminded of Hyde by the school named after him and the two buildings at 1213 and 1400 East Douglas that once housed his Mentholatum factory.

―――――――――
[1] precursor to Century II
[2] today stored at the Wichita Art Museum
[3] northeast corner of Ninth and Hillside

Note: Unattributed quotations in this article were taken from write-ups appearing in the Wichita *Eagle* on March 3, 1925.

Christmas 1925 Ushered In "Buy Now, Pay Later" Scheme

In this age of high tech, high fashion, and (regrettably) high prices, it is instructive to look back at Christmastime in Wichita in the year 1925 – a new age of high tech, high fashion, and the beginnings of credit buying.

Advertisements for electrical gadgets, mechanical toys, and the latest styles in clothing filled the local papers. Catchy slogans and offers of "easy payment plans" lured customers to the stores.

The Kansas Gas and Electric Company was "at your service," fostering the notion that the true spirit of Christmas giving would be best carried out by the purchase of an electrical appliance that would render a service or lighten someone's burden. A small down payment and easy monthly installments made it possible to give an iron priced from $5.00 to $7.50, a coffee pot costing $7.50 to $22.50, a waffle iron at $12.50 to $16.50, and a fan for $7.50 to $9.50. As an added incentive, "packages were gift wrapped, delivered or shipped when desired" by K G & E.

The Vail Jewelry Company (116 East Douglas) offered products of unquestionable quality that could be purchased at low prices on the "Thrift Plan." The plan was originated for the benefit of those who wanted both Vail-quality merchandise and their credit extended longer than a regular 30-day charge account allowed. As the store was ready to explain, "these customers simply prefer to budget their expenditures, and are quick to see the difference between a 'Thrift Plan' at Vail's and ordinary 'easy payment plans.'"

Many stores offered a wide variety of special holiday merchandise, including lavish displays of children's toys. Tanner's (122 North Main) augmented its regular stock of stationery, books, and sporting goods with a fabulous toyland described as "...the most attractive place in Wichita." Stuffed animals sold for 73 cents and doll furniture for 79 cents. Dancing dolls pirouetted on a revolving stand. And, last year's doll could be brought back to Tanner's doll hospital to be repaired.

The Noveltee Store (416 East Douglas) was advertised as "the most interesting gift store in Wichita with something NEW every day," ranging from silhouette pictures, electrical trains, candy boxes, and toy musical instruments to bridge novelties, Christmas tree ornaments, and cards. Especially popular was a new book that featured every comic book character from the Wichita Sunday papers.

"Every little girl wants a cedar chest like mother's" was the slogan used by Lee Lewis Furniture (232-238 North Main) to advertise toy cedar chests costing between $3.95 and $6.00 – with an easy payment plan available, of course!

The Geo. Innes Co. (northeast corner of Douglas and Lawrence[1]) proclaimed: "...everywhere there's the feeling of good fellowship, kindliness and eagerness to serve which characterizes the true Christmas spirit." Gift suggestions included flannelette gowns priced from $1.95 to $3.95; fur-trimmed coats costing $55; fancy clocks with ivory, wood, or leather cases ranging from $2.25 to $8.50; and bonbon dishes for $1.00. It was impossible to leave the store without visiting Toy Town on the second floor. Ives mechanical trains delighted young and old alike; prices ranged from $1.50 to $3.95 for the hundreds of pieces of tracks, tunnels, engines, crossings, etc. Also on display were mechanical automobiles, aeroplanes, boats, firewagons, and much more. Advertising directed at parents urged: "The boy or girl will fairly revel in this department. Bring them up – let them spend an hour or two looking." Customers who could not come to the Innes Co. to shop had only to call the store and ask for Barbara Burney, who would "... gladly attend to your shopping service. Innes is the most satisfactory store in the Southwest from which to buy by mail."

Hockaday's Auto Supply (northwest corner of William and Topeka) claimed that any man or woman would enjoy a gift from their store. Suggestions included motor meters, driving gloves, gasoline coupon books, and just about anything else related to the automobile. That year, Hockaday's also sponsored the *Santa Claus Special* – a 1925 model motor car equipped with 36 automobile accessories, comprising a heater, gasoliter, cigar lighter, ash tray, parking light, tire carrier, tire cover, chains, pump, jack, air gauge, spot light, rim wrench, and automatic windshield wiper. The customer could have all 36 devices for just $278.35! Every day, Santa could be seen "at the wheel," promoting good will along with Hockaday's products as he toured the streets of Wichita.

As was their custom, members of the Kiwanis Club dressed up the shopping and business districts by lining downtown thoroughfares with fresh Christmas trees. On Douglas Avenue from Union Station to the Arkansas River, and on Topeka, Lawrence, Market, and Main from William to First Street, trees were placed 25 feet apart, and merchants illuminated the ones that stood in front of their buildings. The project utilized 800 of the best evergreens available, which were shipped by rail from Michigan, filling an entire box car to capacity and costing the Kiwanis Club $1,000.

And, that was not the only tradition for Kiwanis Club members. They also sponsored a Christmas party for the city's orphaned children. With the help of the Lions Club, they brought children from the Phyllis Wheatley Home, the Wichita Children's Home, the Catholic Orphanage, the Mexican Community House, and the Masonic Home to the Wichita

Forum[2] for a fun-filled evening, which included music from the American Legion Band and two comedy films, *Good Cheer* from Our Gang and *Santa Claus*. Then Santa appeared in person and handed out candy, apples, oranges, and peanuts. There were so many children at the party that it took over two hours to pass out the treats.

Another holiday highlight for the 120 youngsters at the Wichita Children's Home was their overnight stay at the Lassen Hotel. At 5:30 p.m., a street car picked them up and took them to a movie at the Miller Theater. Following the show, the children were taken to the Lassen and treated to dinner in the hotel dining room and a party in the lobby. After receiving Christmas presents and treats, they retired for the night, boys on the third floor and girls on the fourth. The next morning, the children enjoyed a breakfast of scrambled eggs, bacon, and cocoa before being returned to the Home around 10:00 a.m.

Christmas has always been a time for businesses, civic groups, and organizations to help the needy, and 1925 was no exception. Gill Mortuary provided Christmas trees for Wesley Hospital, St. Francis Hospital, and the Wichita Hospital. The Elks and the Masons helped produce the 20th Annual Sam Amidon Dinner[3] at the Wichita Forum, where more than 200 needy persons were fed turkey, potatoes, cranberries, and pies prepared by the Dold Packing Plant. Entertainment was provided by the Durkin Orchestra and several vaudeville acts.

So much more about Christmas 1925 could be described – the entertaining, the school programs, and the church programs. But, this brief account has touched on some important characteristics of the era: an emphasis on technology, the beginnings of credit buying, and the ongoing tradition of caring for the less fortunate.

---

[1] now Broadway
[2] precursor to Century II
[3] continued by Amidon's widow following his death

Wichita has always been proud of its men and women in the armed forces. In the past, particularly after they had served in a war, returning soldiers were welcomed home with a celebration in their honor.

In May of 1919, Wichitans paid a special tribute to all those who had served in the Great War. Many festivities were planned, including parades and feasts. But, the most significant gesture was the construction of a "Victory Arch" across Douglas Avenue at Lawrence[1], which served as a memorial to the city's fallen heroes as well as a greeting to soldiers returning to Wichita.

Planning for the arch began in December of 1918, when a committee backed by Mayor L. W. Clapp was formed in his office to design what was to be a "thing of beauty." Walter A. Vincent, founder and president of Western Lithograph, was designated chairman of the committee and came to be known as "Father of the Welcome Arch." Coy A. Seward, artist and manager of Capper Engraving Company, was appointed secretary.

Glorious Victory Arch Honored World War I Troops

According to plan, the temporary arch spanned 70 feet and reached a height of 40 feet in the center. The abutments at each end measured 14 feet x 21 feet x 31 feet high and were topped with four flagstaffs representing the United States, France, England, and Belgium. The words "For the Liberty of the World" were inscribed in medium gray lettering across both sides of the arch, and a single gold star in the middle "blazoned brightly on the white stucco finish."

Architect for the project was Don Schuler, and the contractor was J. A. Willhite. All of the work was done by Wichita artisans. Sign painters donated their time, and the costs of the undertaking ($5,000) were paid by contributions raised, in part, by the efforts of supporters like Wichita florist C. P. Mueller, who appealed to community pride in urging support: "It will be one of the greatest advertisements the city ever had. Everyone who comes to Wichita will tell of this special arch we have here."

The beautiful Victory Arch was completed just in time for the welcoming celebrations, which began May 8, 1919. The first to arrive was the infantry division on the way to Camp Funston to be mustered out. Their parade began at 9:00 a.m., shortly after the division's arrival at Union Station. Passing under the arch, the troops marched west on Douglas to Water Street and then south to the Wichita Forum[2]. Red Cross nurses led the way, strewing the streets with flowers, and children with baskets threw flowers at the soldiers' feet. Other parade participants were Tremaine's Federated Band; the Spanish War Veterans' Drum Corps, followed by wounded soldiers in flower-bedecked motor cars; and the Fourth Regimental Band of the Kansas National Guard, which had already returned home.

Wichita's 1919 Victory Arch was a sight to behold, but it eventually had to be torn down because it was interfering with traffic on Douglas Avenue.

At the Forum, breakfast had been prepared by the Welcome Home Committee, the ladies of the Eastern Star, and various church organizations. The feast included chicken pie, mashed potatoes and giblet gravy, ham, rolls, cake, and ice cream. Gov. Henry J. Allen and other dignitaries were on hand to greet the troops, and every soldier was given a half-pound box of fudge to take home.

The next day, a repeat of the parade and breakfast was held to welcome the arrival of the field artillery. Mayor L. W. Clapp had proclaimed May 9th to be "Victory Day," stating:

> Every civic and military organization, every commercial and business club, every church, college and school, should join with, and be represented in the committees for preparation of this celebration. An urgent invitation is extended by the city of Wichita to all the people and interests of this part of Kansas, that this day shall be a real gala day; a holiday big enough to be worthy of the cause and the achievements of the army boys and a successful response of the home people to financial demands made upon them.

It was, indeed, a gala day, and over 100,000 Kansans crowded the streets to participate in the victory celebration.

The Victory Arch was dedicated on May 16, 1919, in a ceremony beginning at 9:00 p.m. The dedicatory address, given by W. M. G. Howse, was followed by a spectacular living pictures program. According to the Wichita *Beacon:* "The spectators were held spellbound with the twenty picturesque scenes shown in the brilliancy of the spotlights on the arch panels. Four scenes were shown at a time. More than a hundred persons, men, women, and children, including many overseas soldiers, took part." The pictures depicted the suffering of European countries, with America answering the call, and ended with a peace scene. Background music was provided by the Midian Shrine and Fourth Regimental Bands. "An extra burst of applause greeted the picture that represented the Fourth Victory Loan poster, 'And They Thought We Could Not Fight.'"

As envisioned, the Victory Arch was both beautiful to behold and a monument worthy of the patriotism, heroism, and self-sacrifice for which it stood. Committee chairman Walter Vincent was "told by others who have seen welcome arches in different cities, that Wichita's arch stands as one of the most magnificent and beautiful ... of any they have seen." Still, it was not meant to last forever, and a year after all of the troops had returned home, the remarkable arch was but a memory.

---

[1] now Broadway
[2] razed to make way for Century II

Note: Unattributed quotations in this article were drawn from the Wichita *Beacon's* coverage of the Victory Arch campaign and the May 1919 dedication ceremonies.

In 1934, Many "Danced Off" Their Thanksgiving Dinner

A look back at Wichita's Thanksgiving celebration of 1934 shows how some Thanksgiving traditions have endured over the years, while other customs once associated with this holiday have disappeared.

The traditional union church services that year were held at four locations: First Presbyterian, Wellington Place Baptist, St. James Episcopal, and Calvary Methodist. Religious and charitable groups saw that hundreds of destitute families were fed. Even the prisoners from the city jail and farm were paroled so they could spend Thanksgiving Day with family and friends.

Wichita schools offered a variety of plays, programs, and special activities in honor of the occasion. Miss Aileen Lee's fourth and fifth graders at Franklin Elementary wrote and presented a playlet, then served a feast consisting of foods that the Pilgrims would have eaten: samp porridge, wild turkey, maple sugar cookies, cranberries, oysters, fish, and deer. The kindergartners at A. A. Hyde Elementary, under the supervision of teacher Miss Dorothy Anderson, baked pumpkin pies and invited their mothers to join them for dessert.

Wichita High School East students participated in a radio broadcast over station KFH. Superintendent L. W. Mayberry introduced the program, which featured a mixed chorus of 160 voices, an orchestra, and talks by two students, Miss Joan Williams and Earl Stuckenbruck, on "What Thanksgiving Means to Me."

The Recreation Hall at Friends University was the site of a varsity Thanksgiving dinner for students, faculty, and friends sponsored by the home economics department. Entertainment included speeches, recitations, games, and singing. Leona Binford and Otho Cott portrayed Mother and Father Penn; Dr. and Mrs. David M. Edwards and Dr. and Mrs. Henry Fellows were special guests.

With the big band era in full swing, and ballroom dancing all the rage, combining a dance and Thanksgiving dinner was a popular form of celebration in 1934. Among the formal dinner dances held in Wichita that year was the one hosted by Mr. and Mrs. Earl Duke, Mr. and Mrs. Russell Jump, and Mr. and Mrs. Homer Fox at the Crestview Country Club, where guests danced to the music of Virgil Lauck and his orchestra. An equally elegant affair held at the Wichita Country Club featured the Bond-Turner Orchestra.

The Broadview Hotel Roofgarden was the site of two holiday dances, including the one held on Thanksgiving Day sponsored by Sigma Phi Gamma Sorority. Hal Newman and his orchestra provided music for dancing, and Miss Mossie Stuckey, Mrs. Harry Howard, and Miss Sue Stewart were hostesses for the evening. A partial reservation list printed in the local papers revealed that at least 28 misses and 28 messrs. planned to attend the event.

The other, held on Thanksgiving Eve, was called "the season's biggest entertainment treat." The four-star show featured James Hall along with blues singer Valjean Aldred, the Masquers Quartet, and, again, the Hal Newman Orchestra. Admission to this dance was 75 cents per person.

At the Wintergarden (217-1/2 West Douglas), described as "Wichita's most popular ballroom," tables could be reserved free, and guests could dance to the sounds of Clarence Love and his orchestra.

The Wintergarden Ballroom, c. 1934.

Tiny Little's sensational orchestra furnished music for the dance held at the Palms Ballroom (1805 East Second). Ads for the gala celebration read:

> Doubling forty-three different instruments,
> with novelties galore. DON'T MISS IT.
> Dancing Nine till One.

For the family, local theaters offered a variety of entertainments. *Anne of Green Gables* was showing at the Palace, along with Pop-Eye the Sailor Man in *Dance Contest*. The Uptown Theater offered the perfect Thanksgiving treat aboard the good ship Hispaniola: *Treasure Island*. But the ideal holiday program for the whole family was *The Pursuit of Happiness* at the Miller Theater. Local papers advertised this show as "a page left out of our school histories. We inherited the Puritan's Thanksgiving and pumpkin pie – but somehow we missed out on Bundling – the nicest little Puritan custom of all – it's the last (or first) word in cold weather courtin' – and if practiced today, it would save a lot on our gas and coal bills."

In 1934, just as today, football was a part of Thanksgiving Day. Fans rooting for their home teams saw Friends University defeated by Southwestern College 14 to 0, and Wichita University[1], playing at Topeka, defeated by Washburn 6 to 0.

And, let's not forget the food! For those desiring to prepare Thanksgiving dinner at home, the Wichita *Beacon* estimated it would cost $4.19 to feed a family of six. That figure was based on the following menu: a 12-pound turkey (at 17 cents per pound), oyster dressing, mashed potatoes and gravy, green beans, celery hearts, olives, Parker House rolls, cranberry jelly, cloves, fruit salad with whipped cream, fruit cocktail, pumpkin pie, and coffee. Readers who thought the meal sounded expensive were reminded that "Thanksgiving dinner is one occasion when no one minds the cost. At least, the drumsticks are free!"

Those preferring to eat out could have turkey and all the trimmings for $1.00 at the KitKat in the Allis Hotel, for 50 cents at the Holly Cafe (119 West Douglas), and for 60 cents at the Lincoln Cafeteria across from the Miller Theater. Or, they could dine at the Innes Tea Room and enjoy special music by the Californians with guest Guy Gaylen, "formerly of the Hollywood Roosevelt Hotel." But, reservations at the Tea Room had to be made early, because seating was limited.

---

[1] now Wichita State University

Note: Unattributed quotations contained in this article appeared in issues of the Wichita *Eagle* during the 1934 Thanksgiving season.

People thought there was something a little odd about William Boulton — and there was. "A married Pony Express rider with four children," was the way Herb Brame described Boulton in his article for the *Pony Express Courier* in November 1935. What's more, he sang on the job!

An American legend, the Pony Express celebrated its 136th anniversary on April 3, 1996. But 58 years before that, in 1938, Wichitans paid tribute to Boulton, whose grave at Highland Cemetery[1] was located through the efforts of the Oregon Trail Memorial Association and Boy Scout Troop #30 of the Kansas Masonic Home.

William Boulton: No Ordinary Pony Express Rider

William Boulton was born in England in 1828. When he was five years old, he and his parents emigrated to Canada, where he grew up on a farm and became interested in horses and cattle. In 1856, he left his family in Canada and rode horseback to eastern Kansas to become a scout and Indian fighter.

When the Pony Express was organized in 1860, Boulton was hired by Colonel Majors as a pony rider and given a run between Seneca and Marysville in the Eastern Division. Conscientious and dependable, he was known as a rider who always came through. On one occasion, his horse was injured in a fall about five miles from Guittard's station. Boulton gathered up the scattered letters, put them in the pouch, and traveled the five miles on foot. At Guittard's station, he resumed his journey on a fresh horse.

Boulton became famous for singing on his route, while waiting at express stations for other pony riders. He was also known to repay favors with a song or two. Mrs. Perry Hutchinson, whose reminiscences of the singing Pony Express rider were contained in Brame's article, recalled Boulton stopping at her home "for a drink of water from the cool spring at their cabin," which was located about seven miles east of Marysville. He was so thrilled with a piece of her freshly baked gingerbread that he sang several songs, including *Sweet Alice* and *Ben Bolt*, to her and the children. Many times after that, Boulton stopped at the Hutchinsons' house for doughnuts or cakes and repaid them by singing his "sweet-voiced songs." Mrs. Hutchinson believed without a doubt that Billy Boulton was the most popular rider on the entire route.

But, he was certainly not typical of the Pony Express riders. Most all of them were young, single boys. Boulton did look younger than his 32 years, and he did lead Colonel Majors to believe he was single. But, there was always the question of why he "never seemed to lean toward any of the girls that had 'set their hat' for him around Seneca." The question was answered when Boulton took a month's leave in 1861 and went up to Canada to get his wife and four children!

After the Pony Express services discontinued, Boulton took a job as a bullwhacker in Seneca, Kansas. He was soon elected sheriff – "the only Democrat ever elected in that county for the office" up to that time. Boulton came to Wichita in the late 1890s and died here in 1899.

On Memorial Day, May 30, 1938, at 10:00 a.m., Wichita citizens gath-

Pony Express Riders meeting on the plains.

Wells Fargo Pony Express stamp.

ered at Highland Cemetery to honor William Boulton. Scout Troop #30 and the Scout Masters placed an American flag, a pony riders' flag, and flowers on his grave. There was a prayer, a eulogy of his life, and a recitation of the Pony Express riders' pledge. A salute of gunfire ended the ceremony.

Present that day were Boulton's grandson Charles and his wife; their daughter, Margie, and their son, Jimmy, and his wife. During a 1991 interview with the author, Margie Boulton Fairleigh and Mr. and Mrs. Jimmy Boulton recalled the 1938 ceremony with fond memories. Mrs. Boulton particularly remembered the parade before the service.

---

[1] Wichita's pioneer cemetery, northwest corner of Ninth and Hillside

Note: Unattributed quotations in this article were taken from the article by Herb Brame in the November 1935 issue of the *Pony Express Courier*.

Charles Boulton Shared "Close Shave" with Radio Audience

"How does it feel to be stretched out on a cold slab in the morgue, entirely paralyzed except for your mind, and listen to [the] undertaker's assistants discussing your imminent embalmment?"

That was the question Charles Boulton[1] answered on Floyd Gibbons' CBS Radio broadcast *Your True Adventures* on Thursday, February 25, 1937. Thousands of Wichitans were tuned to KFH at 9:00 p.m. to hear the story of his incredibly close call.

Boulton gave a vivid account of that unforgettable day in 1907 when he was a lineman for the Wichita Gas, Electric Light and Power Company. He was secured by his safety belt atop a power pole in the 200 block of East Douglas, working on the dormant line used for the nighttime power of 2300 volts, "when suddenly my right hand froze in a powerful grip around a wire."

Now, if the high voltage was to be switched on for any reason during the day, company procedure required the plant engineer to be notified. He, in turn, was to sound a signal on a whistle to alert the linemen, then wait ten minutes for them to clear the line or call in for more time.

On the morning in question, a meeting was scheduled at the Masonic Temple. There wasn't enough light in the building, so Mason James Walsh, who was also the superintendent of the power company, "and who could have more light if he demanded it, phoned to the plant for the engineer to turn on the 2300 [volt] circuit, and not to wait to whistle, as there was no one working on it and they wanted light right away."

That's when "I received the full benefit of the 2300 volts," Charles explained to his radio audience. I "was on it some time before the rest of the crew could get to me, and ... lowered me off the pole with a rope."

Boulton recalled being taken to a nearby doctor's office, "and after working on me for quite a little while, he pronounced me dead." All the time he lay in the morgue, Charles said, "... I was perfectly conscious, with my eyes closed, not able to wink an eye, or say a word or move a muscle. ... It was not until they were all ready to embalm me that I could move even an eye, but as they were bending over me, to start, I felt my eyes gradually opening. The undertaker noticed it and a doctor was called, and I was revived and sent to a hospital."

Although Boulton recovered, the scars from the severe burns on his hand and leg remained with him for life. When he returned to work after spending about six weeks in bed, Boulton found that the electric company had elevated him to the position of foreman.

Coincidentally, two years after and four blocks west of Charles Boulton's accident, his brother William, also a lineman, was on top of a power pole on West Douglas and died when "his hand came in contact with a wire carrying 2300 volts of electricity."

Moreover, Charles himself survived a second near-electrocution a few years later: "Knocked unconscious in a similar manner while working in Tulsa (for the street railway company), Boulton ... quit his position ... returning to Wichita, where he took up the prosaic life of a cobbler."

For years, Boulton operated a shoe repair business at 2314 E. Douglas. He later moved the shop to 3109 E. Central. But his quiet, uneventful life as a shoe repairman came to an end when he submitted his story to Floyd Gibbons' contest

Beginning in 1925, KFH Radio was housed in the Lassen Hotel. The station's call letters were based on a "Kansas Finest Hotel" promotion conducted soon after the Lassen opened in 1919.

and won $25 in prize money — plus an expense-paid trip to New York for the radio broadcast that dramatized his brush with death.

Boulton's thrilling adventure was also published in the "Floyd Gibbons Adventures Club" column of the New York *Evening Journal*. As a result, he gained national fame and received letters from people all over the nation inquiring about his story.

When Gibbons was given a contract with Vitaphone Corporation to film some of these "Adventures," Boulton's experience was dramatized as a Warner Brothers two-reeler entitled *Danger! High Voltage*. It was awarded second prize by Warner Brothers, and Boulton was given a second free trip to New York to accept the award. He appeared in person along with his "short" when it played in Wichita at the Orpheum Theater.

In 1938, a scant year after his adventure was aired, Charles Boulton died. He is buried at Maple Grove Cemetery[2].

[1] grandson of singing Pony Express rider William Boulton
[2] northeast corner of Ninth and Hillside

Note: Unattributed quotations in this article appeared in the Wichita *Beacon* on August 17, 1909, and February 24, 1937, respectively.

Wichita's City Flag Displays Indian Symbols, National Colors

"Who can do for Wichita what Betsy Ross did for the United States?" That was the question put before the American Legion in 1937 by City Manager Bert Wells. He was speaking on behalf of civic-minded Wichitans, who for some time had felt the need for a city flag to display during parades and other gala occasions.

In response to their plea, Craig Kennedy, commander of Thomas Hopkins Post of the American Legion, appointed a civic flag committee composed of Paul Henrion, secretary-treasurer of Henrion Improvement Co., chairman; H. M. Van Auken, secretary of the Chamber of Commerce; Glenn Thomas, architect; William H. Allen of the Spencer-Allen Fuel Company; and John Rydjord, University of Wichita professor. The committee was assigned the task of planning and conducting a design competition and recommending to the City Commission that the winning entry be adopted as the official City of Wichita flag.

Everyone was eligible to enter the competition, and there was no limit to the number of entries an individual could submit. Ideas, suggestions, and designs were to be submitted by written description or actual drawing, either in pencil or ink, on uniform size sheets of paper (8-1/2 inches x 11 inches). The name, address and telephone number of the person submitting the idea was to be enclosed in a sealed envelope; no name was to appear on the drawing or idea itself. For purposes of identification, the outside of the envelope containing the contestant's name was to bear a duplicate or copy of the design or idea entered by that person. All entries were to be submitted to the American Legion headquarters at 335 North Topeka before 6:00 p.m. on May 25th. Any and all ideas, suggestions, or designs entered in the contest were to become the property of the American Legion.

More than 100 entries were submitted, 13 of them by one person (S. Raymond Jocelyn). Judges for the contest were Wichita artists William Dickerson of the Wichita Art Association and Charles Capps and Robert Aitchison, both American Legion members. Although there were many good designs, the judges agreed that a design entered by artist Cecil McAlister was the one that best symbolized Wichita (an American Indian word meaning "scattered lodges").

Simple, but rich in Wichita's Native American heritage, McAlister's design depicted Indian motifs rendered in the national colors. To the left of center, a white ring encircled a blue sun, a symbol of happiness for the people of the city. In the center of the blue sun was a white sun circle, the Indian symbol for hogan or "permanent home." Alternate red and white stripes radiated from the white ring – the red designating honor and the white symbolizing courage.

For his effort, Cecil McAlister won the $40.00 first prize. The other five winners were Ted Hawkins, second prize ($25.00), Ruth Gaynor, third prize ($10.00), Lillian Simpson, fourth prize ($5.00), Ray H. Elliott, fifth prize ($3.00), and Gertrude Martin, sixth prize ($2.00).[1] The Rotary Club of Wichita furnished the $85.00 in prize money, which was distributed to the six winners at a Rotary luncheon held at the Lassen Hotel.

In a resolution signed by Mayor T. Walker Weaver at the City Commission meeting[2] held on Flag Day, June 14, 1937, the winning design by Cecil McAlister was adopted as that of the official City of Wichita flag.

Unable to find a commercial flag manufacturer, Wichita produced a "modern Betsy Ross." She was Mary J. Harper, whose skillful and well-trained fingers fashioned the 6-foot x 9-foot flag from red, white, and blue silk. On July 23, 1937, it was flown over the City Building[3] for the first time. Businesses were urged to display the new city flag along with the Grand Old Flag when they decorated the streets in front of their establishments. Exactly how many flags Mrs. Harper finally made is not known, but records show that she made at least five more.

Although no original official city flag is flown today, the mass-produced ones can be seen throughout Wichita and on various occasions and at special events. One is displayed in the City Commission meeting room. Others are flown over

19/1 postcard view of the official flag, City of Wichita, Kansas.

City Hall, Century II, and the median of Douglas Avenue between Main and Market. The Wichita-Sedgwick County Historical Museum has one in its possession. During the Wichita River Festival, a city flag is flown on the West Bank. The Henry Helgerson Company still sells them to action groups needing a new flag to fly. And, at one time, City Hall was giving out colored postcards of the flag and small lapel pins in the shape and colors of the flag.

---

[1] The 5th and 6th place winners were actually Ted Hawkins and Cecil McAlister; since they had already won 1st and 2nd prizes with other designs, Elliott and Martin moved up to 5th and 6th place.

[2] At this same meeting, the petunia was designated as Wichita's official city flower. It had been recommended by the Wichita Park Board and the Wichita Garden Club.

[3] today the Wichita-Sedgwick County Historical Museum

Wichita Boathouse Makes a Spectacular Comeback

Wichita's handsome new Boathouse, which was dedicated on April 21, 1994, under the auspices of the Arkansas River Foundation, marks the return of an enchanting Wichita tradition; and, to those who remember the old one, it brings back fond memories.

The story of the Boathouse began nearly a century ago, when, in 1898, R. C. Israel gave some wooden rowboats to his sons, Robert, 14, and Carl, 10. They kept the boats on the bank of the Little Arkansas River, just south of the Murdock Street Bridge, and rented them out on Sundays for 25 cents. The new attraction proved so popular that the boys had to rent boats out in the evenings as well, and they soon had a thriving business. Wichitans could take the street car to the Murdock Street Bridge and rent a boat or canoe, or walk across the bridge into Riverside Park.

In 1905, a storage facility and clubhouse for the newly-established Wichita Canoe Club (whose members owned a total of 250 canoes) was built on the site. Business continued to boom, and in 1907, a new 25-foot launch was purchased. When the season opened on June 12th, ads in the Wichita *Eagle* read: "The Riverside Boat House and Refreshment Parlors. Music provided by Bamberger's Orchestra. Ice Cream Pavilion Over Water Where It's Cool. Boat Prices Same as Always. A 35 minute trip in the launch, 'Bessie May,' 10 cents. Parties and picnics get rates on either launch or row boats."

R. C. Israel retired from the real estate business to devote full time to the Riverside Boat Company, and the enterprise became a family affair. For many years, the Israels invited youngsters from the Wichita Children's Home and the Kansas Masonic Home to the Boathouse to enjoy a day on the river complete with refreshments. In 1911, R. C. stated in the *Eagle:* "It would have done your heart good to have been at Riverside Saturday night to see the children." Fifty orphans attended events at the Boathouse that day.

The same year, the Boathouse received 22 new pressed steel boats, of which two were motor boats of the largest pattern, making 45 in all with two to four seats. At that time, Mr. Israel told the *Eagle,* "We do not hesitate to invest a good deal of money in this business. The city commissioners did a great thing for the people when they built the dam and placed the sand boat[1] in the river. We are going to have one of the prettiest rivers in the west and you will see hundreds and thousands of people enjoying it. Instead of a stream with a stinking mud bottom we are going to have a clean channel with clear water.

Photo of the Riverside Boathouse, c. 1910.

(far left) Photo of the four-story remodeled Riverside Boathouse, c. 1925.

1996 photo of the new Wichita Boathouse on the east bank of the Arkansas River at Lewis Street.

The boating will simply be out of sight." Catchy advertisements in the local papers said that boating in the morning was the most delightful way to enjoy nature and encouraged people to get out and try it.

Each year, the annual opening of the Boathouse was a gala event, and 1916 was no exception. Approximately 3,000 people attended the event that year. Automobiles were seen everywhere, even blocking driveways near Riverside Park, and the river was a sight to behold! The Wichita Girls Band played while spectators watched the dozens of decorated canoes and 86 rowboats which the Riverside Boat Company now owned, along with the three large launches. Water craft could be seen everywhere along the river. The Wichita *Eagle* reported: "The feature of the evening was the spectacular dive of Ed Ball, a Wichita diver, who leaped from a 65-foot ladder into a flame of fire. Gasoline was spread upon the water and was touched by a match just as the diver leaped. The electric lights were put out as Mr. Ball made the dive, and the spectacle of a scantily clad man jumping from a high ladder into a mass of flames leaping high into the air brought the spectators to their feet."

A new image was seen in the 1920s – a four-story Boathouse with columned verandas overlooking the river, and a concrete bridge to replace the old steel bridge. The unique semicircular observation bays on the new bridge made an attractive place to stand and watch the boats.

In 1924, R. C. Israel and his wife, Julia, were reminiscing for the *Eagle* about how they had built the Boathouse many years ago both for their family's pleasure and to give the boys a summer job. "From that time to this, the boat house on Murdock avenue has grown more popular as a place to while away idle time, and the canoe club has grown apace." Israel died a few months later, and Julia took over the business. Following her death in 1935, it was managed by other family members.

For years thereafter, visiting the Riverside Boat House and participating in its many activities remained a favorite recreational pastime for families and dating couples. In addition to the leisurely canoe ride, there were boat races, dances, and thrilling high-diving exhibitions.

In 1954, the Israel family sold the boathouse, which continued operating until the 1960s. Sadly, the building was condemned in 1965 and razed by Urban Renewal in 1968. For the next 25 years, this unique facility would be missing from Wichita's recreational scene.

Today, however, the boats are back! Thanks to the Arkansas River Foundation, the Boathouse lives on – at a different location and for a new generation.

---

[1] a steam-powered dredge which suctioned sand from the river in order to deepen the channel